BUSINESS VISIBILITY

MINDSET SHIFTS TO HELP YOU STOP PLAYING SMALL, DIMMING YOUR LIGHT AND DEVALUING YOUR MAGIC

HOLLY E. WORTON

CONTENTS

A CIP catalogue record for this book is available from the British Library

ISBN 978-1-911161-51-6 print
ISBN 978-1-911161-52-3 EPUB
ISBN 978-1-911161-53-0 MOBI

Published by Tribal Publishing Ltd

Please direct permissions requests to:
permissions@tribal-publishing.com

"Your playing small does not serve the world. There is nothing enlightened about shrinking so that other people won't feel insecure around you. We are all meant to shine, as children do. We were born to make manifest the glory of God that is within us. It's not just in some of us; it's in everyone. And as we let our own light shine, we unconsciously give other people permission to do the same. As we are liberated from our own fear, our presence automatically liberates others."

— Marianne Williamson, *A Return to Love*

INTRODUCTION TO THE SECOND EDITION

This book was originally published in ebook format only, back in 2016. I quietly released it to my email list and my social media followers. I didn't do much else in terms of marketing or advertising. Sales were okay, and I know that the book did reach many people beyond my audience because I get emails from readers all the time.

Since then, I've gone on to do *a lot* of mindset work with myself around visibility. My 2019 book, *If Trees Could Talk: Life Lessons from the Wisdom of the Woods* (yes, a complete departure from my business mindset books) is a collection of stories from trees that I received throughout 2018. Yes, you read that right: I talk to trees. And they talk back.

It was important to me to get this book out in a big way, and that meant hiring a book launch manager who promised to get the book on at least one Amazon bestseller list (in the end, she got me to number one on *sixteen* lists) and a publicist, who got me coverage in a national newspaper in the UK and also on live television in the UK.

None of that would have been possible without the mindset work that I've done over the years. I talk a lot about the spiral staircase of mindset work: with one step we do the mindset work, with the next step, we take practical action toward our goals. And that's how I've been working with myself—step by step—since even before I wrote this book.

I was even doing mindset work on the train into London before my appearance on ITV This Morning. Here's a sample of the kinds of things I was balancing for:

- I accept criticism with grace and ease.
- I feel neutral when I receive criticism.
- I feel calm and confident in my message, even in the face of criticism.
- I feel confident in my message even when people contradict me.
- It's safe and appropriate for people to contradict me.
- It's my job to make "woo" normal.
- I'm ready, willing, and able to make "woo" normal.
- I'm ready, willing, and able to talk about channeling in a big way.
- I'm ready, willing, and able to be seen as a weird person.
- I'm ready, willing, and able to take a stand for what I believe.
- I'm ready, willing, and able to be of service to the trees.
- I'm ready, willing, and able to be of service to Source.
- I'm ready, willing, and able to be seen in a big way.
- I'm read, willing, and able to go BIG.

The result? Friends who watched the show told me that I came across calm and confident in my message, very natural, and very much as I am off-camera. I read mostly positive things when I browsed through the comments on social media for This Morning.

Of course, there were also negative comments. Some people thought I had a mental illness; others thought I was seeking attention. Do you know how I felt about that? Calm and neutral. I didn't take it personally. It didn't hurt. I didn't get that energetic punch to the gut that I've felt in the past when reading negative reviews of my books. I didn't take it personally.

The shift was massive. And it set me up for the next level of visibility. All the work I did made it possible for me to go up a level on the spiral staircase of visibility.

On the way home from my live television appearance, I was on such a high from the experience, that I spent the entire ride home doing more mindset work. I wanted to attract more experiences like that in my life, and I wanted to be sure I was ready for it.

Do you know what happened? That live television appearance led to me being invited to appear on BBC Radio Scotland and other talk radio shows. A couple of months later, I was invited to record a clip for ITV, and less than a year later, they asked me back for This Morning, this time sending me halfway across the country on location. This stuff works.

I wanted to share this story so you can see: no matter how much work I do, if I want to keep growing, I keep taking action, and I keep doing the mindset work. For me, it's a never-ending process. I don't do the mindset work every day; instead, I'll do it when I feel it's needed. I may do some work with myself every day for three or four days, and then nothing for a couple of weeks—or even months.

But I'm always aware of whether I need to be doing any work or not.

This is what I want for you: to have a clear vision of where you want to go, what you need to do to get there, and what you need to believe about yourself to take action. That way, you'll more easily be able to get to where you want in your business (and life!).

In this book, I'm going to talk about what business visibility is and how it can affect all the different areas of your business. We're going to look at the power of visibility, and how that fits into your big vision for your business. Then, we're going to explore your beliefs, blocks, and fears around being visible. Finally, we're going to look at how to do the mindset work to transform your fears, blocks, and limiting beliefs into supportive, enhancing beliefs that will help you to get visible in a bigger way.

INTRODUCTION TO THE FIRST EDITION

I'm so excited to be taking you on this journey with me. I'm going to help you explore your beliefs around visibility and how they affect your ability to market your business and get it out there to your ideal clients.

Visibility is one of the fifteen categories of business blocks that I included in my two previous business books: *Business Beliefs: 600+ Beliefs That Make Up a Successful Business Mindset* and *Business Blocks: How to Identify and Release Your Blocks to Create a Successful Business Mindset*. This book delves deeper into one of the most important facets of business mindset: visibility. The first two books serve as a useful introduction to this one, but you can read the books in any order you like.

I chose visibility as the first category to delve deeper into because it's one of the biggest signs that we need to upgrade our business mindset. It's one of the most stubborn issues I've had to deal with in building my own business as a solopreneur, and it's one of the most common themes that my clients bring to work with me.

They say that you teach what you most need to learn,

and it's no surprise that I tend to attract clients with visibility issues. It's been a massive hurdle for me to overcome in my business, and my word of the year for 2016 was Shine. That was my way of reminding myself of my commitment to increasing my business visibility by shining my light. I even painted a small canvas with glittery paint, and hung it on the wall behind my desk as a constant reminder of this commitment to shine.

Visibility blocks are usually very easy to spot, and often come in the form of things that we procrastinate on. When we have fears and blocks around visibility in our business, we tend to avoid those actions that serve to make us more visible, which pretty much includes everything in the area of marketing and sales. And when we avoid marketing and sales, we become the best-kept secret in our field, blocking clients from coming in because no one has ever heard of us.

This is how visibility blocks show up in business:

- You'd love to be one of those big name motivational speakers, and you've got a great story to tell that would really inspire your ideal clients, but you're terrified of public speaking... so you just don't do it.
- You know how important it would be to create a YouTube channel full of videos that express your personality and how you can help people, but you hate the sound of your voice and what you look like on video. Plus, commenters on YouTube can be horrible, and you're scared of negative feedback on your videos. That's why "start a YouTube channel" is still on your to-do

list, and why it keeps getting pushed farther and farther down the list.

- You enjoy writing and you know you have a book in you, but you haven't even bothered to explore the possibility of actually writing a book because the thought of writing one is so scary. Who are you to call yourself an author? What if you get bad reviews? Your writing surely isn't good enough for a book. Better to just dream about it.
- You avoid business networking like the plague. You hate standing up to do your one-minute elevator pitch, and you even cringe at the thought of having individual conversations with people in the informal networking that goes on before and after the main meeting. You really struggle to express what you do in a coherent way, so you've decided to just avoid networking for now.
- You dabble in social media marketing, but you're afraid to do too much of it. After all, you don't want to be one of those obnoxious people who fills up people's Twitter feeds and Facebook timelines with their posts. You hate the thought of getting in people's faces with your business. Better to just post every once in a while.

Do any of these situations sound familiar to you? Perhaps you've experienced one or more of these situations, or maybe they've reminded you of other ways you play small and hide in the shadows, both online and offline. By hiding from your ideal clients and lurking in the darkness it's almost like you're striving to win a medal as the best-kept secret in your field.

Playing small is often a result of business mindset blocks in some or all of the following areas (if you've read one or both of my previous books, you'll recognize these from the fifteen categories of business mindset): action and goals, change and growth, confidence and self trust, leadership, personal power, success and opportunities, and value and self worth. When we have blocks in these areas, they can affect our ability and willingness to put ourselves out there and market our business in a bigger way.

The root cause behind our visibility problems often has to do with fears, blocks, and limiting beliefs. Getting clarity on what these blocks are is the first step to transforming them. When we are able to access these issues and get clear on exactly what's holding us back, then we know what we're working with.

And when we know exactly which aspects of our business mindset need to be changed, then it's just a matter of choosing *how* we want to transform those beliefs. This is a simplified description of how to make it happen, but believe me: it's that easy. I know because I've done it. And I make it happen every day with my clients.

That's why I've written these books: to help you get clarity on the specific things that are holding you back from growing your business. And because clarity is just the first step, I'll also share with you how you can transform your beliefs and release your visibility blocks.

1

PURPOSE OF THIS BOOK

> "You are going to often find that to step into your biggest opportunity, you will be asked to move through your biggest fear or insecurity."
>
> — Ali Brown

I have three main intentions for this book. First, that it will help you identify and overcome the fears, blocks, and limiting beliefs that are holding you back from being more visible with your business, both online and offline. Second, that it will tell you what you need to know so you can transform your business mindset. Finally, that doing this mindset work will help you more easily take action toward being more visible with your business. I want you to shine (and to feel comfortable doing so)!

There are two main aspects of being visible with our businesses: there's the practical business and marketing side of things, and there's the mindset part. When we struggle to achieve our business goals and create the business and lifestyle of our dreams, the problem usually doesn't have to do with learning more about business (that's easy enough—there's plenty of information and programs out there to teach you about business). It's often the mindset stuff that's holding us back: all of the fears, blocks, and limiting beliefs that make difficult for us to take action toward our goals.

Because the mindset part is the hidden part, most people fail to address their business mindset early enough on their business journey, and instead focus on the practical work. They also spend much of their time learning: about the skill they offer as a service, about business and entrepreneurship, and about sales and marketing. In reality, I believe that we need to be constantly working on both: upgrading our mindset as well as taking action toward our goals (which sometimes involves learning new things). It's a two-step process.

Our business mindset is made up of our fears, blocks and beliefs—both supportive beliefs and limiting beliefs. I discuss business beliefs in depth in my first mindset book, *Business Beliefs*, which teaches you how to tap into your subconscious mind and identify which beliefs you hold at the subconscious level. It introduces the fifteen categories of business mindset that I mentioned earlier, and it shares a list of over 1,000 business beliefs that can help you to upgrade your business mindset. If you want to learn more about business beliefs, it's an excellent companion book to this one.

My second book, *Business Blocks*, explores the shadow side of business mindset and helps you to uncover the blocks that may be holding you back in building your business. It's another super actionable book that will help you dig deep to discover which aspects of your business mindset need to be upgraded. Because it explores all of the fifteen categories of blocks (one of which is Visibility), it's a good companion to this book. Sometimes, our visibility is affected by other things, like fears around growth, blocks around confidence, and limiting beliefs around personal power.

What you want

But first things first...let's focus on *you* for a minute. And let's start with the end in mind. What exactly do *you* want to get out of reading this book? What are *you* hoping to achieve?

Stop reading for a minute, think about this, and then write down your answer somewhere. It's important to know what you want to get out of this book, because it means you'll be more likely to achieve it. It's also important to write it down, for three reasons:

1. It helps you to clarify your vision, goals, and plans
2. It helps you to commit to these
3. It helps you to see whether you have achieved these goals once you've finished reading this book and implemented what you learned

It's my intention that this book will help you to dig deeper so you can explore what's making you play small and preventing you from taking your business out to a bigger audience. The deeper you dig to discover your blocks, the more likely you are to find the core of the issue that's stopping you from having that dream business today. Sometimes it can be uncomfortable, but it's rewarding work.

You're in the right place if:

- Something isn't quite working in your business, but you're not sure what. You've had great results with the few clients that you've had, but it seems to be feast or famine, and you haven't yet been able to tap into a steady stream of clients.
- You've got enough clients for your low cost online course, but you can't manage to get enough people onto your VIP program. You know you've got to put yourself out there in a bigger way, but you just haven't managed to do it.
- You know you could get your business in front of your ideal clients if you just believed in yourself more.
- You're willing to take an honest look at what might be holding you back from making yourself more visible, both online and offline.
- You're ready to take action to transform your business visibility.

As with my previous two business mindset books, I've intentionally kept this book fairly short and focused so you can use it as a quick, practical reference to transform your business visibility, and not get caught up in lots of theory. This book is about getting clarity fast, and then taking action on what you've learned. I'm a big believer that *you* know what's best for you, so I encourage you to use this book in whatever way you find most useful.

If you have any questions, please get in touch via my website: www.hollyworton.com.

Below is a list of related podcast episodes. I've been

producing a weekly podcast since 2013, and it's full of useful resources that will help support you on your journey to visibility and personal growth. Most episodes now have downloadable transcripts, so you can read as you listen, or instead of listening.

On the podcast

You can find the full list of podcast episodes here: www.hollyworton.com/podcast

- 215 Holly Worton ~ Boost Your Visibility With Reviews, Testimonials, Referrals, & Shoutouts (now with downloadable transcript!)
- 213 Holly Worton ~ How to Face the Shadow Side of Visibility With Confidence (now with downloadable transcript!)
- 211 Holly Worton ~ How to Redefine Visibility & Create Deeper Connections Online (now with downloadable transcript!)
- 157 Holly Worton ~ How to Increase Your Visibility by Transforming Your Mindset
- 137 Holly Worton ~ How to Stop Hiding & Overcome Your Fear of Visibility (now with downloadable transcript!)
- 53 How to Raise Your Visibility, with Jenny Kovacs

2

ABOUT ME

"Your intuition knows what to do. The trick is getting your head to shut up so you can hear."

— Louise Smith

If you've read my previous books, *Business Beliefs* and *Business Blocks*, you can skip most of this chapter. It's the same story. I've included it here for readers who haven't yet read those two titles and have purchased this book first. You can head straight to the end of the chapter, and answer the questions in the Take Action Today section.

For many years, I was a business mindset coach for women entrepreneurs. I worked with women who were feeling stuck and frustrated because they felt like they were hitting a plateau in their business. Maybe they were struggling to get a steady stream of clients, or perhaps they wanted to grow their business to a new level. My work was to help them release their fear of visibility, set aligned prices for their products and services, and take inspired action to grow their business.

Today, I've taken a step back from one-to-one sessions so I can focus on my writing. I've learned a lot from my years of coaching and mindset work with clients that I want to share in a more significant way through my books.

I'm dedicating this chapter to sharing my business journey with you so that I can clearly explain how changing my mindset has completely transformed my business and my life. That way, you'll understand *why* I do what I do: business mindset has been one of my biggest life lessons. My life—and business—can be divided into two phases:

1. Before I discovered mindset work
2. After I discovered mindset work

It's also crucial for me to tell you my story so you can get an idea of just how powerful it is to change your business mindset at the subconscious and energetic levels. I went from a place of having extremely low confidence and low self-esteem to being sure of myself and proud of what I do. Mindset work is profound work, and it can create significant results in very little time.

I know what it's like to struggle to build a business on my own. That's why I worked in the field of business mindset for so long. I know how it feels to be doing all the right things, and yet not achieve my goals. And I know what it's like to experience significant changes once I started doing the mindset work by transforming my beliefs at this profound level.

My first company

I've been an entrepreneur since 1999. My first company, which was in the hospitality industry, was a constant uphill struggle as I learned new business and marketing skills. I was in a state of continual learning and expansion, which was both exciting and exhausting. I had quit my graduate studies in literature at UCLA to start the company with a business partner in Latin America.

Despite having zero experience in hospitality, my business partner and I managed to build a wildly successful business. We went from four small cabañas on the beach to owning and operating three ecological hotels in southeast Mexico, with a second property in development in Patagonia, and a central office in Buenos Aires that managed sales, reservations, and marketing.

Our hotels in Mexico were cutting edge: we were the first in the area to embrace and promote the concept of eco-travel, and we were the first to create a holistic spa featuring local Mayan healers and massage therapists. The resort was such a big part of our business that we used to say we had a "spa with hotels" rather than "three hotels with a spa."

We were a media darling. Editors from significant travel and spa publications came from all over the world to feature our properties. International celebrities came to stay with us—some returning for a second or third visit.

My primary role in the company was in the area of online marketing. We built our first website in 1999, and I soon started using pay-per-click advertising on Goto, which later became Overture and eventually Yahoo! Search Marketing (this was long before Google AdWords, or even Google, for that matter). Our marketing was also cutting edge compared to other hotels in the area. We fully embraced technology—despite being located in the jungle—and we focused our efforts on driving traffic directly to our website. We consistently brought more than 80% of our reservations, drastically reducing costs because we didn't have to pay much in travel agent commissions.

The business also spread and grew through word of mouth. One evening, I was hanging out near the front desk and asked a guest how they heard of us. To my surprise, he told me that he had been at a party in San Francisco and had met someone who had just returned from our hotel. They were so effusive in their praise that the man went straight home and booked a stay with us.

We regularly heard from guests about how their lives had been changed by their holiday at our properties. Our seaside cabañas were candlelit, surrounded by native jungle, allowing guests to disconnect from their day to day hustle and enter a state of deep relaxation and recovery from stress. We had created something unique, and other hotels within the region began to copy us. These copycats were hoping to recreate our success.

It was both thrilling to receive such attention and attain such great success. It was also deeply satisfying to have created a unique experience that helped people in a significant way. However, there was another side to this phase of my life.

The inner journey

My business partner and I were very different people, and we had very different skill sets and levels of entrepreneurial experience. For me, it was my first company, and for him, it was just one in a string of companies he had owned and operated. I threw myself into the operation of the business from the start, and I immediately felt out of place and overwhelmed with what I was doing. I felt very, very unqualified to be an entrepreneur.

I was learning new things on a daily basis, and I was implementing what I learned immediately after. Some aspects of the business I learned as a result of doing things the wrong way: I learned from my mistakes. It was 1999—the early days of the internet—so there wasn't as much information available then. It was a massive growth period for me, one that went on for the ten and a half years I ran the business with my partner.

The company was in a constant state of growth and expansion, and that meant the same for me. It was hugely transformative on a personal and professional level, but also incredibly frustrating and exhausting. I'm very grateful for the experience because I learned so much about business and marketing, but it was indeed a trial by fire.

Besides, my business partner and I had very different values, and he made decisions based on his values that regularly conflicted with my sense of integrity. I found myself in a position where I allowed him to make decisions for the business that felt entirely out of alignment for me.

The shadow side

There was also a shadow side to this experience: my partner. My business partner wasn't a great person. I'm no psychiatrist, but he fits the profile of someone with narcissistic personality disorder. He was also a workaholic and demanded that I follow his example in working long and exhausting hours. He engaged in gaslighting, a tactic in which one person makes someone else question their reality, usually to gain control or power over them.

While I was busy at work co-creating and marketing this beautiful healing refuge for our guests, I also heard things like:

- *"You're so stupid. You're not even smart enough to be a secretary."*
- *"You're worthless."*

- *"You never do anything right. When anything goes wrong, you should just automatically apologize, because it's probably your fault, even if you think it's not."*

It was confusing because part of me knew that I was doing great work and getting great results in our business. The feedback I was getting from my business partner didn't correlate with the reality I was seeing. But because I heard things like this day in and day out, over the course of ten years, I started to lose touch with reality. I began to question what I was seeing. I stopped trusting myself, and I began to believe the things I heard at a very deep level.

These statements, and many others like them, seeped into my subconscious mind and adversely affected my beliefs. They set me up with a mindset that would negatively affect my future business ventures and make it very, very difficult for me to build a successful business on my own. It's been over a decade since I left that partnership, and I've taken that long to undo the damage. I'm still working on my healing. This stuff went in deep.

The disconnect deepened

Eventually, I became so disconnected from myself that I had no idea which way was up, in terms of my internal compass. The gaslighting had me completely disoriented. So many things felt wrong, and I felt so lost that I didn't know how to get myself out of the mess I had created for myself.

Ten and a half years later, when I quit running the company, I was so lost and out of touch with myself that I didn't know what I wanted. All I knew was that I couldn't take it anymore. I no longer wanted to be running a business with my partner, even though I dearly loved the people who worked for us, and I felt terrible about abandoning them, which was how I saw it at the time.

A new beginning

Eventually, I left. In 2008 I moved out, and almost a year later, I quit the business. It was one of the hardest decisions I'd ever had to make. I had co-created the company from scratch, and I genuinely cared about the business and the people who worked there. But I knew it had to be done, for my own mental and emotional wellbeing.

Around the time I left my company in 2009, I met my husband. With his help, I started to realize I wasn't the stupid, useless person I believed myself to be. I also began to understand just how bad things had been for the past ten years of my life. I had lost all perspective on how I deserved to be treated by others.

After quitting my first company, I took an extended sabbatical, which ended up lasting almost a year and a half. I took time off to heal, rest, and recover. I also spent the time trying to figure out what I wanted to do next. I knew I had lots of skills, but I wasn't sure what to do with them.

Near the end of the sabbatical, we packed up everything and moved to London, where I trained as a coach and as an NLP (Neuro-Linguistic Programming) practitioner. I was so excited to run a business where I could help people once again, albeit in a very different way. I was very enthusiastic about my new skills, and I was confident that I was on the right path.

I started with a life coaching business, helping women to find their life purpose. It was tough, and I struggled to get clients, despite knowing what I needed to do to start a business. Out of all the other coaches I trained with, I was the only one who had a decade of practical business and online marketing experience. I knew what to do, and I was putting it into action, but for some reason, my company just wasn't working.

After several months of struggle, I heeded the advice of a business mentor. I settled into a social media marketing company, where I used the skills in online marketing that I learned in my very first company to help authors learn to use social media for marketing their books online. This business later evolved into helping women solopreneurs with social media. But it still wasn't easy.

The struggle

I was making enough money to support myself and to pay the bills, but it was a constant struggle. Building my business was *so damn hard*. There was no sense of ease and flow. It was all push, push, push to get minimal results. It was exhausting and disheartening.

If my first business was a lesson in practical business and marketing skills, my solopreneur adventures have been a lesson in business mindset. In Tribal Publishing and Socially Holistic, the names of my social media companies, I learned for the first time about the *other* kind of struggle that happens in business—the one that very few people discuss. (Tribal Publishing started out providing social media services and consulting for authors and only later evolved into what it is today: my own publishing company, which also provides publishing services to authors.)

In my new companies, I was no longer part of a large organization; I was a solopreneur, and my company was all about *me*. I didn't have the confidence to step into my greatness and shine brightly with my new business endeavors.

On the contrary: I shrank into the shadows, crippled by

my smallness. It felt like I was taking one step forward and two steps backward with my marketing. I was trying to put myself out there, but *not too much*. I was playing it safe—safe inside my comfort zone. It all felt so vulnerable.

For the first time in my life, I battled my inner mindset gremlins—lack of confidence and low self-esteem—as I struggled to build my social media business and get clients. New fears, blocks, and limiting beliefs reared their ugly heads daily. I believed I wasn't good enough, and that I wasn't worthy of having a successful business. It felt crippling.

And the worst part of it was that I had no idea what was going on. I just thought that I needed to take yet another online marketing course (despite having ten years of experience in the area) or hire another coach or business mentor (despite already knowing what I needed to do). I believed those things would fix all my problems. I struggled, and I pushed, and I put in so much effort, but I didn't get much in terms of results.

A light in the darkness

I was entirely in the dark about what was going on: that my mindset didn't serve me one bit. It was full of fears and blocks and limiting beliefs that kept me stuck. I was also struggling with personal issues that weren't shifting no matter what therapies I tried.

A friend of mine eventually recommended that I train in a process that he was using with his clients: PSYCH-K®. This process helped me quickly and easily change my subconscious beliefs. It was a simple process that helped me to easily communicate with my subconscious mind so I could change the beliefs that limited my self-esteem, my relationships, my business performance, and even my physical health. I used it to transform *every single aspect of my life.*

I started where everyone starts: with the Basic Workshop, and I used the process daily with myself. The results were so quick and precise that I attended the Advanced Integration Workshop, and later the Pro (which has since evolved into the Master Facilitation Workshop). Not wanting to miss a single workshop, I traveled to the US to attend the Health and Wellbeing Program, which completely transformed my physical health and wellness.

When I find something that works, I throw myself into it completely. After using this process regularly for over a year, I went back and did all the training *again*. This time, I was able to absorb the little details that made much more sense after more than a year of working with this process regularly. It deepened my understanding of beliefs and how I worked with them, and it made me a much better facilitator. I was settling into my mindset work, both with myself and with clients.

Big life changes

This process was life-changing. It lifted me from a place of stuckness and struggle and transported me into a place of ease and flow. The more I used it, the easier things became.

My mindset dramatically shifted to a more positive, uplifting state. Tasks that I had previously procrastinated on suddenly became easy to complete. Working through my to-do list became easy, rather than a constant struggle. Reaching out to joint venture partners, something which used to terrify me, was instantly simple. Setting up Facebook ads to reach a larger audience, something I used to balk at, became easy. Being visible in my business felt natural, rather than terrifying.

I know this sounds too good to be true, but here's what was happening: I was no longer sabotaging my efforts. That alone made everything so much easier. So many of the things that used to hold me back became easy to take action on. And as a result of taking these actions, my business grew, and it was easier to get clients to sign up for my products and services. Things started to flow with ease.

This process was so hugely transformational for me and my business that I knew I had to start using it to help others. I added it to Socially Holistic, my social media company because so many of the women I worked with had inner struggles around their online marketing. They either believed they weren't tech-savvy, or else they were afraid of being visible online in a big way. Or both. I used to say that I helped people with social media from the inside and out. Not only did I teach them practical techniques and strategy, but I also helped them to release the blocks that kept them from using this strategy so they could step up in a more significant way.

The more I worked with women on the inner side of online marketing, the more I realized that this mindset work was my favorite part of my business. It was the most fulfilling part of my work, and I decided it was time for me to transform my business once again. It was a big decision, but I was confident that I was on the right path.

Big business changes

I decided to let go of the technical aspect of Socially Holistic and revisit a brand I had built a few years back when I first trained as a coach: Ready to Bloom. I had always loved the name, and it perfectly fit the work I was doing: helping women solopreneurs transform their business mindset so their business could bloom. I wanted to help as many entrepreneurs to be successful in their businesses as I possibly could.

In 2016, I rebranded once again and let go of the Ready to Bloom brand. As much as I loved the name, I felt that it was time for me to stop hiding behind a business name and step up into my personal brand. I was the central part of my business and the work that I did, and it was time to make that apparent through my business name. I'm positive that it was my mindset work that led me to that point. It had once felt safe to hide behind a business brand, while now it felt limiting. It was time to step up and *just be me.*

Interestingly, this decision came just one month after I released the first edition of my *Business Beliefs* book. Writing and publishing my first business mindset book was yet another significant step in terms of business visibility and claiming my spot as an expert in the field of business mindset. It was a big, scary step, and it triggered lots of hidden limiting beliefs for me to work on.

"Who are *you* to write a book about business mindset?" demanded my mind gremlins. But I did the mindset work, I released the fears and limiting beliefs, and the book went out. Since then, I've received fantastic feedback on all of my business mindset books.

Heart-centered Energy Work®

In late April 2016, about the same time, I was rebranding my entire business, I received a message from my spirit guides via my business mentor, Lisa Wechtenhiser. Spirit guides are energetic beings that include angels, ascended masters, ancestors, elementals, and spirit animals or power animals. Essentially, they're spirits that have the ability and desire to help us and guide us in life.

Lisa calls herself the "trust whisperer," and she's been

an essential part of my journey to stepping into my power and trusting my intuition. She's helped me to step up in a much bigger way. I come away from each session with her with lists of mindset work to do on my own. Lisa also calls herself "practically woo" because she channels your guides as she delivers practical business advice. This two-pronged approach to business is super powerful.

In this particular session, the guides chimed in to inform me that I was experiencing a significant upgrade, like a door opening. They told me that I was about to experience a shift in terms of what I did and how I helped people to transform their mindset. They urged me to make a list of which aspects of PSYCH-K® felt right to me, and which parts didn't.

They asked me to look at what I most resonated with, and what wasn't me. The guides suggested I explore how I currently blended these things, and to consider whether maybe there was a new way to do my work. They said that it was time for me to find what that worked for me—something new.

The spirit guides told me that I needed to create my process. They asked me to put together a list of ingredients and to metaphorically put them into a mixing bowl and stir them up. They said that the process I would eventually use with clients would look very different.

They were right. I went away and made my lists, and I spent most of 2016 with the plan to create a new process. I intuitively knew that it would be something that I would receive as a kind of information download and not something that I would create rationally. And so I waited for it to happen.

And I waited.

It was a long process, and there was a bit of struggle, mainly because I simply didn't make the time and space for it to come through. But eventually, in late 2016, over the course of just five days, I channeled the new technique that I later used to help clients with their business mindset. It's called Heart-centered Energy Work®, and it helps to not only transform beliefs at the subconscious level but also to release any energy blocks at the same time.

It's quick and powerful, and it gets excellent results for both my clients and me. The critical point for me to make here is that I would never have been able to channel this profoundly transformative technique if I hadn't done the mindset work to get myself to a place where I believed I could do it. I believed in myself, and I knew I had the power to receive this information, but only because I had previously done the mindset work to reprogram my beliefs.

Author-entrepreneur

And then, in late 2018, I decided to quit my business mindset work to focus on my writing. This change felt like a risky move. I worried that people wouldn't take me seriously. I stressed that people would think I was flaky—yet again. But I knew that I loved writing, and I wanted to focus my work on helping a wider audience. That would be much easier to do by writing books, rather than filling my calendar with one-to-one sessions.

Since my first book, *Business Beliefs*, I've written and published another nine full-length books, five short reads books, and three workbooks. And I've continued to grow from there, not just as a writer but as an author-entrepreneur and independent publisher. Not only that, but as you saw in my Introduction to this book, I've stepped up in a big way in terms of visibility. I'm no longer afraid to be open and vulnerable and tell my story in my books, and then market it to a much wider audience. In fact, I've been investing a lot of money in advertising to help my book reach people who have probably never heard of me before.

I've been there

As you can see, I've come from a challenging place: one of extreme lack of self -belief and self-confidence. I know what it's like to feel frustrated not to have all the necessary pieces to have your business work. I know what it's like to focus on the practical side of the business and to ignore the mindset work completely. I know what it's like to struggle. And I've come out the other side.

That's why it was so vital for me to tell you my full story: so you could see how far I've come in just a few years. I ran my first business from 1999 to 2009 and started my coaching journey in 2011. It wasn't until mid-2013 that I started to focus on my mindset—that's less than three years before I released the first edition of this book.

That's not much time, considering how far I've come in terms of mindset. I went from being in a very, very dark place to release my smallness and stepping into my greatness. I let go of the mind crap that was holding me back, and I adopted new beliefs that served me better.

And then it all came together: my coaching training from back in 2011 has helped me to help my clients dig deep and to get clear on what's currently holding them back and what they want instead, so we can start transforming those beliefs quickly and effectively. My work with authors in my first social media business in 2012 has given me the tools and knowledge to help people through my books, such as this one. And my extensive mindset work, which I began in 2013, got me to the place where I believed in myself.

This process all sounds straightforward in retrospect because I can now look back on the past few years and see how it's all come together seamlessly. But there were some murky bits, which I hope that I clearly expressed when telling my story because I believe that it's essential to look at the shadow side of things. The deeper we dig, the more valuable the treasure we will find.

When I speak of treasure, I'm referring to two things: first, the core limiting beliefs that, once shifted, will unlock and transform all the other limiting beliefs that hover near the surface and are often easier to spot. One of my PSYCH-K® instructors called this "finding the diamond." We can work much more quickly when we're willing to dig deep within ourselves to get to the root of an issue.

The second part of the treasure is clarity. A lot of my work—first with one-to-one clients, now with my books—involves helping people get clarity on exactly what it is that they *do* want so that we can program that intention into their subconscious. Once you have a clear vision for your business, and once you believe that you're capable of achieving this vision, the easier it will be for you to take practical action to make it happen.

Now that I've shared my business journey with you and you can see the power of mindset work, we're ready to talk about the power of beliefs, the power of the subconscious mind, and the power of energy work. Because that's where we often get stuck, and that's where the real magic can happen, once we know how to do the work and get out of our way.

Take action today

Before we get into the next chapter, I'd like to encourage you to write down *your* story. Start wherever you want: you can begin with your first job in high school, or your lemonade stand as a child (I had an orange juice stand). Get into the details when you relate your business journey: what were all the different iterations of your business? What did you do? How did you help people?

Most importantly, how did you *feel* at all the different stages of your entrepreneurial journey? Were you afraid people would find out you were a fraud? Were you afraid you weren't good enough? Did you always compare yourself to other entrepreneurs with a similar business model? What were your fears and beliefs about yourself and about your ability to run a successful business? What are your current fears and beliefs?

How did these fears, blocks, and limiting beliefs affect your ability to be visible with your business? On a scale of 1 to 10, with 10 being highest, how visible would you say you are today with your business? What would a 10 look like to you? What would you need to do to get there? What would you need to believe about yourself to make it happen? What's stopping you from doing this?

3

WHAT IS BUSINESS VISIBILITY?

"A star does not compete with other stars around it; it just shines."

— Matshona Dhliwayo

First of all, what is visibility? It can be defined as how clearly objects can be seen, or how far you can see clearly, or the degree to which someone sees something. Therefore, business visibility is how clearly the public can see you and your business, how far and wide your business is known, or the degree to which your ideal clients see you and your business.

Why is visibility important? Because you can be the best professional in your field, but if no one has ever heard of you, you won't have a single client. Your business will be nothing more than a hobby, and it will never get off the ground. Sadly, this is the story of most small businesses. Many business owners start with big dreams and fail to achieve them.

If you've been playing small, then you probably have

low business visibility. The concept of "playing small" was popularized by author Marianne Williamson in the quote I shared at the start of this book. That most likely means that you've been struggling to bring in a steady stream of clients, because your ideal clients may have never even heard of you. Playing small means giving in to your Smallness, rather than stepping up into your Greatness.

When we stay stuck in our comfort zone without stepping out of it, we're playing small. When we shy away from activities that make us visible, like speaking engagements, we're playing small. When we avoid sales calls with potential clients, we're playing small.

Low visibility entrepreneurs often struggle to explain precisely and coherently what they do and fumble over their words when delivering their elevator pitch at a networking meeting. That's because they're fearful of being seen when they stand up to talk about themselves. Being a low visibility entrepreneur can be awkward and difficult. But the reality is that most people probably don't even notice because, as you may have guessed, they don't remember having come across the low visibility business owner.

Contrast this with high visibility entrepreneurs, the big-name women in business. In the business coaching/mentoring world, the names Marie Forleo, Leonie Dawson, Natalie Sisson, and Denise Duffield-Thomas come to mind. These are the entrepreneurs who have thriving communities around their business. They have a raving tribe of fans who love what they do and look forward to their next podcast episode, blog post, or YouTube video. And I can guarantee you that they have a steady stream of clients.

You may or may not have heard of them, but if you haven't, I'm sure you can come up with a few names of highly visible entrepreneurs outside of the online. Oprah, maybe? Arianna Huffington, Sara Blakely, and Estée Lauder also come to mind (yes, Lauder was an actual person, not just a brand). Whether or not you're a fan of these entrepreneurs, there are plenty of people around the world who love their products and services.

Your business visibility is directly related to your income because if no one has ever heard of you, they won't be able to hire you. It's that simple. I know because I've been there.

I'm going to run through my fourteen of my fifteen categories (the last one is Visibility) and give you some examples of what low visibility can look like in your business. Some of these may apply to you; others may not. But they may trigger an understanding of how you're blocked and stuck in terms of visibility in each area of your business.

Action and Goals

You avoid taking the steps you need to take to be seen with your business. Maybe you blog or podcast, but then you don't share those blog posts and podcast episodes online, so no one hears about them. You can count the number of blog readers and podcast listeners on both hands—and you can probably name all of them too because they're your friends and family members. No one outside your inner circle knows who you are or what you do because you're not taking the right actions to make that happen.

This was me for so long. I was creating loads of content: blog posts, podcast episodes, and videos. I *did* share them on social media, but I wasn't working to grow my audience, so not that many people saw the things that I spent my valuable time producing. I was visible to a tiny audience. And I struggled to grow that audience for a long time.

Why? It felt scary and vulnerable to share my content with a broader group of people. What would they think of me?

Change and Growth

You've been stuck in the same place for weeks, months, maybe even years. You've been complaining about the same things for ages: you don't have enough clients, you're not selling enough books, you're not making enough money. Your email list is the same size (or, worse, it shrinks every time you send out an email, and people unsubscribe), your website visitors are the same as they've always been, and your podcast episodes are still getting the same downloads. Nothing's changed, and you haven't grown. Nor has your business. Your visibility has stagnated.

The email list is a personal example. I cobbled together a list many years ago, and for the longest time, I was terrified to send out emails more than once a month because I didn't want to bother people. I also went months on end without ever sending anything to my list, because I didn't want my list to get smaller if I sent out a newsletter and people unsubscribed. I was stuck at a particular number of subscribers, and I was too paralyzed to use my list, so the numbers I did have served no purpose.

I felt so stuck and frustrated for so long in my business. I tried working with coaches and business mentors, but I still didn't get the results I wanted. I wasn't getting visible. It took lots of mindset work for me to be able to take the actions I needed to take to get more visible. I did the work, and little by little, I started changing into the person I needed to be to choose the right actions.

Eventually, when I released my book *If Trees Could Talk* in 2019, I hired a book launch manager and a publicist, and that's when I was able to get visible in a much bigger way. This was a huge tipping point for me that was only possible because I had done the inner work. That was a significant tipping point for me that allowed for much bigger growth and change in my business.

Clients and Boundaries

You either have a handful of clients or none at all. And the clients you do have are all people that you're doing exchanges or session swaps with: they're other healers or service providers that want what you have to offer, but they're not willing or able to pay for it. The same goes for you. You're not visible enough to get the client load that you want for your business.

I spent some time like this. I offered several people a free session in exchange for a testimonial, and then it took me ages to get out of that habit. I justified it by telling myself that I was getting much-needed practice in the service I was providing. I was honing my technique! But really, I felt safe with my practice clients—I wasn't charging them actual money, so I wasn't at risk of them complaining about the quality of my services. In this way, I avoided getting valuable feedback on my offering. It was safe!

What helped was getting a placement on the website for the healing modality that I was working with at the time—that opened me up to a whole new audience of people who had never heard of me before. It was scary, but it worked to grow my business and get paying clients. However, I wouldn't have had the confidence to do so without first doing the mindset work.

Confidence and Self-Trust

You feel like a fraud. You've been faking it until you make it, but you haven't made it yet, and you're terrified that someone will find out that it's because you have no idea what you're talking about. You're an imposter, and your impostor syndrome is keeping you invisible.

Self-confidence has always been a big issue for me. I've often felt like a fraud—like I wasn't good enough to do whatever it was that I was doing. I wasn't good enough to help people with social media, I wasn't good enough to help people with business, and I wasn't good enough to write these books. The fact that I received excellent feedback on my work wasn't enough to convince me otherwise. And so I continued to play small.

"I'm not good enough" has been *the* overarching limiting belief that has underpinned all the other fears, blocks, and limiting beliefs throughout my life.

After doing the mindset work to boost my self-confidence and self-trust, I slowly began to believe in myself. I felt more and more confident. I was able to do my work with ease, trusting that I had the skill and knowledge to do the things I was doing in my business. Finally, I felt good—I believed in myself.

Maybe you're also struggling with self-confidence, and you believe you're not good enough to do the work that you do. Lack of confidence can affect the decisions you make in marketing your business, which can lead to playing small and low business visibility. Self-confidence and professional confidence are linked to visibility blocks.

Creativity

You have plenty of ideas, but you do nothing with them. You don't blog, you don't podcast, and you don't create videos for your YouTube channel. You don't create content. Maybe you don't even have a website. Your creativity blocks are keeping you from being visible in the world.

This isn't an area that I've struggled with; I've always been a creative person. My issues with creativity aren't about being unable to create things like podcast episodes or books, but rather about believing that my creations are good enough to publish. I've always enjoyed creating podcast episodes, blog posts, and YouTube videos. It was putting them out there that was difficult.

But doing the mindset work made it much easier for me to create these types of content and release them out in the world. It especially made it easier for me to share them online, and promote my creations so people would actually find out about them, rather than quietly publishing them and then forgetting about them.

Leadership and Outsourcing

You're busy, busy, busy, filling your days with admin work. There are many things to do when you own a business, and you're doing all of them. You've heard of such a thing as virtual assistants, but you know deep down that no one else would do things as well as you do. Your leadership and outsourcing blocks keep you so busy that you don't have the time to do the essential tasks that will get you visible.

I haven't always been a leader, but I certainly learned to be in my first company. Yet I never saw myself as a leader until recent years. There were many situations where I stepped up as a leader, yet I couldn't see this quality in myself. And so I failed to step up to many opportunities that would have led to increased visibility.

Outsourcing is something that I thankfully haven't struggled with as much. Because I had so many employees in my first company, I had plenty of experience delegating tasks and managing people. However, in my coaching business, I often failed to hire people who would specifically help me to uplevel my visibility—until, of course, I hired that publicist who changed everything for me.

And after much mindset work, I was able to see myself as the leader that I already was. I was able to step up in a more significant way and shine my light out into the world. I was able to allow myself to be seen as a leader.

Learning

There are so many things to learn when you start your first business. And there are so many things to learn even when you're an established business owner—that is if you want to keep innovating. Many people have blocks around learning new things, especially technology. And there's plenty of technology in any business these days.

I've always been a good learner, so I didn't have many blocks around my ability to learn new things. I have, however, allowed learning to get in the way of me doing more important things. My "addiction to learning" has led me to sign up for classes that I don't need, which makes me waste time on online courses instead of doing the things I need to do to get visible.

I have seen plenty of clients struggle with learning in their business due to previous trauma in the early years of school. At some point, a teacher or authority figure told them they weren't a good learner, and they took on that belief for themselves.

I have also seen many clients get stuck in learning mode: continually upgrading their skills, and learning more about business than doing the things they need to do to get visible. They learn about sales and marketing and never implement what they've learned. But they feel like they've made progress because they've completed that online course.

If you've got learning-related trauma, doing work to release past trauma can be incredibly healing. We can't delete the experience from our memories, but we can remove the associated trauma. This is a straightforward technique that you can accomplish using processes like PSYCH-K® or TRE (Trauma Release Exercises).

Lifestyle

You quit your job to run your own business, but now it seems like you're working harder than ever. Sometimes we trade our job for an even harder one. The only difference is that now *we're* the boss, but we're working even longer hours than before. But that doesn't mean we're working on our visibility.

This was a significant problem for me in my first company: I lived in paradise, but I couldn't enjoy it because I was working from 8 am to 1 am every day. I was ridiculously stressed out, despite owning and operating a resort and spa. I was working hard so that other people could relax.

When I started my various solopreneur ventures, I went the complete opposite direction and became very careful about how I spent my time so that I could avoid burnout. It wasn't only after much mindset work that I was able to find a happy medium, where I could work intensely and get things done, and then take time off to relax.

Other people are afraid of significantly increasing the level of their lifestyle because they'll surpass their friends and family. What will they think? And so they avoid getting visible with their business, so they don't have to worry about friends and family thinking they're a snob because they have such a great lifestyle.

Marketing and Sales

Marketing and sales (or lack of activity in these areas) are also indicative of the types of visibility blocks you have. Marketing is all about putting your business out there to connect with potential clients, and sales is all about getting clients on board to work with you. It's that simple. If you've got issues with either of these areas, that will affect your business visibility.

You hate marketing, and you're terrible at sales. You're terrified of asking for money for your services, and you don't want to be one of those annoying and pushy salespeople. You avoid business networking like it's the plague; you hate those ridiculous elevator pitches people are expected to give. And so you stay stuck in your Smallness, refusing to get visible and step into your Greatness.

In my first company, I was great at sales and marketing. I had a great product (ecohotels) and offered excellent services (food, spa, accommodation). It was an easy sell! And it wasn't about me.

But when I began my first small business as a solopreneur, it was hard for me to market myself. It just all felt too personal. And so I played small and kept my visibility low. I didn't seek out lots of discovery calls to get new clients. I avoided sales conversations. I didn't advertise.

Despite having ten years of experience in online marketing, I struggled to market myself online when I first set up as a coach in 2011. It was *so hard.* I knew all the things I was supposed to be doing, but I wasn't doing them. Or I'd take action, but not do a good job, and it would come out looking and sounding incredibly awkward because I'd forced myself to do it. I had loads of visibility blocks.

After much mindset work around marketing and sales, I improved in marketing my services—and my books. For my ninth book, I was able to hire an excellent publicist, who got me on national television in the UK, which brought me so much more visibility than I had experienced before. I'm aware that I keep bringing this story up, but it's a perfect example of how one different action can change everything.

Money

Business owners with low visibility often struggle to bring in a consistent amount of money each month, experiencing spurts of income and then dry spells. That's because they haven't yet made an impact on their potential clients. They may take isolated actions that bring in clients—like giving a talk—but they aren't doing it on a regular enough basis to leave a lasting impression on anybody.

I have had significant money blocks ever since my first company. Before that, I was an excellent custodian of money: I made money, I saved money, and I invested it in having great experiences, like when I studied abroad in Spain in university. But my business partner in my first company was ridiculously bad with money, and that infected me with poor money management practices that I have since struggled to unlearn. Not only that, but he was financially abusive (a concept that I didn't understand until many years later), so I had a lot of trauma to heal around money.

Little by little, after much mindset work around money, I improved. I started bringing in more and more money from my company and my books, and I've got a much better handle on how I manage it all. I feel more confident, and I'm proud of how far I've come, after a decade of poor money practices in my first company.

Personal Power

You feel small and unimportant. You'd like to do great things in life, but you don't believe that you can. You see online influencers and online business gurus, and you know you could never be like them. You silently follow them and observe how they do things, hiding in their shadows.

Personal power is your sense of freedom, groundedness, and personal responsibility. It's about standing firm and taking responsibility for yourself, your actions, and your thoughts. It's about guiding your life in the direction you want to go and engaging with life and other people and things in the way you want. It's about showing up in the world as the real you and creating the life that you want.

Personal power is multi-layered. It is made up of the layers of self-awareness, self-trust, self-love, self-acceptance, self-esteem, self-confidence, self-respect, self-worth. It's about power from within, not power over others.

When we don't feel strong and powerful in what we stand for with our business, it can lead to wanting to play small and hide. When we genuinely believe that we can make a difference in the world with our work, that belief can blast through many visibility blocks.

Having a strong sense of personal power can boost your visibility. But if you suffer from low self-trust, low self-esteem, and low self-confidence, you're more likely to stay stuck in your Smallness, avoiding opportunities to be visible.

I have often felt powerless in my life. I have shied away from standing in my power and speaking my truth. I have regularly watered down my message. I have often toned down my true colors until I looked like a murky shade of beige, trying painfully to fit in everywhere.

Mindset work has helped me to stand out. It's helped me to say yes to media opportunities, even when I knew I'd be criticized for my beliefs. It's helped me to write these books and others, and share my unfiltered experiences with readers. It's helped me to be vulnerable and step into my personal power.

Strategy, Clarity, and Vision

You have no idea where you're going with your business. You know what you like doing, and you want to do that thing. How are you going to make money doing it? Who knows. They say that if you do the job you love, the money will follow—won't it? You have no strategy and no clear vision, so you don't know what you need to do to be visible.

After I left my first company, I had no idea what I wanted to do with my life. I had so many skills, and I had learned so many things, but I had no idea how to apply that to my life. I was so out of touch with myself that I didn't even know what I wanted to do.

Eventually, I ended up on the coaching and personal development path, which led me to my mindset work and finally to where I am today, living life as an author-entrepreneur and independent publisher. At each iteration of my business, I had a clear vision and strategy, which I continued to refine along the way. I adjusted the details and pivoted on my path, and my vision became more and more refined. This was all in thanks to the mindset work that I did, which not only gave me the clarity but also allowed me to act on it and become visible in increasingly bigger ways.

Success and Opportunities

Opportunities occasionally come your way, but you don't always take them. They're not quite right, you know? And you certainly don't feel successful. And because you don't feel successful, you don't take action to get visible and therefore achieve the success you dream of. It's a downward spiral.

For *years* I felt unsuccessful. I kept working hard, and putting in the hours, and doing the mindset work, and I still wasn't seeing results. It was disheartening, and I thought I'd never make it. There were many times where I felt utterly hopeless. I kept comparing myself to others, and that only served to bring me down even farther.

But I kept at it. I persevered and refined my vision and strategy, and eventually, I started to feel things shift. Opportunities started coming to me, and I kept saying yes. And then, there was a turning point. I began to feel successful.

This was all possible thanks to the mindset work that I was doing to help me get clarity on what success looked like to me. I did the work to ensure that I saw opportunities when they arose. And I changed my beliefs so that I was able to accept those opportunities when I saw them.

Value and Self-Worth

You *think* you're good at what you do, but so are a lot of other people. Your prices are low because you want to keep them reasonable, and many of your clients are quite honestly friends that you're doing swap sessions with. You're not good enough to charge more.

If we don't value our skills, products, and services enough, it can lead to us feeling like our business offerings aren't worth much. This can lead to not wanting to stand out with our business because we're terrified someone will come along and say we're just not worth what we're asking for our work.

Someone once told me a story of a woman who finished her training and was excited to get clients. But she didn't value her skill, and she didn't value her time. So she took out an ad in a local publication, advertising sessions for £30 an hour. Not long after, she got her first client.

After their session, the client tried to pay her £300. The coach protested. There was a misunderstanding—and there was. The publication had made a misprint and had advertised her services at £300 an hour, not £30. The client insisted that the coach take the £300, which was ten times her usual rate because the session had been well worth it. And, the client stressed, if she had thought the session would cost £30, she wouldn't have called—she would have assumed it was a cheap, shoddy service by someone who was either very unprofessional or unskilled. The client valued the coach's skills more than the coach did herself.

Value and self-worth have been some of my biggest lessons. This has been one of the most significant areas that I've worked on in terms of mindset. "I'm not good enough" is my default shitty place that I go to when I'm feeling down. It's the motto of my mind gremlins. It's the phrase that comes up whenever I do something new, or step up in a more significant way. *I'm not good enough.*

Not surprisingly, this is one of the beliefs that has come up most often with clients. Many, many new entrepreneurs struggle to believe that they are good enough: they're good enough to provide their services, they're good enough to charge appropriate fees for their services, and they're good enough to ask for referrals to get new clients. This is an essential core belief for every business owner: *I am good enough.*

After much mindset work, things started to shift in this area for me. It was something that I had to keep coming back to, as I peeled the layers of lack and low worth and went deeper and deeper with my mindset work. I can't say that I'm 100% there yet (it keeps rearing its head every once in a while), but I've experienced massive shifts in terms of how I value myself. And to be honest, as I grow, I expect to trigger this belief many times more. It's a sign that I'm up-leveling, and things are changing.

Take action today

Go through each of the 14 categories and write down at least one way in which you're experiencing low visibility in your business. If you can think of more than one example for each category, write them all down. This will help to give you a clear idea of how low visibility is showing up in your business today.

4

THE POWER OF VISIBILITY

When you have high business visibility, it's easy for your ideal clients to find you online or offline, because it's easy for them to see you or hear you. Maybe you've got a popular podcast, with tens of thousands of downloads each week. Perhaps you've got a wildly successful YouTube channel or a popular blog. However it is that you get yourself out there, it's easy for people to find you.

With high business visibility, it's easier for you to make an impact and leave a lasting impression on people. Even if they aren't ready to work with you at this time, for whatever reason, they'll have you at the forefront of their mind when they are prepared to work on whatever it is that you help people with. That's because you've got high visibility, and you're always around. It's hard for them to forget you.

When you're a highly visible entrepreneur, it's easy for you to speak about what you do and to talk about your business compellingly. You're confident, and you're used to putting yourself on stage to speak, whether on a webinar, at a big conference, or a local networking group. You're visible, and you express yourself clearly.

When you're visible with your business, it's easy and effortless for you to take up space, both online and offline. Taking up space may involve creating Facebook ads, so you're more visible there, or it might include speaking at an upcoming event. This is all about being physically present, whether it's with your body on a stage or with pixels on a computer screen.

The good news is that, while it does take time and effort to build up your business visibility, it's not an impossible task. You don't have to work long, hard hours, though you do have to put in the time. The key to making it easy is to identify and release your visibility blocks and get clear on what you want instead.

Here's what high visibility can look like in your business:

Action and Goals

You have a clear vision of how you want to be visible, and you take action to achieve this. Your goals are bigger and brighter every year, and you're excited, rather than scared, of working toward them. You take easy, inspired action by doing the things you need to do to get visible in a much bigger way.

Change and Growth

You have a big vision for your business and life, and you know you'll have to change and grow to achieve it. You're willing to step into the unknown as you expand and grow into your dream. You know that you're going to have to change and grow to get visible so you can get from where you are to where you want to be.

Clients and Boundaries

You have a steady stream of ideal clients. You may even have a waiting list! You only take on the clients you know are right for you, and you do not hesitate to turn people down or recommend another professional to them if you know you're not a good fit. After all, you have more than enough clients to fill your calendar. This is all possible because you got visible in a big way.

Confidence and Self Trust

You feel confident in your ability to achieve your goals and dreams, and you feel confident in your ability to provide excellent products and services to your clients. You trust in yourself to do all the things you need to do to make your vision a reality, so you easily step up and become visible so that you can build your business.

Creativity

You love expressing your creativity through your business. You write blog posts and books, you record videos and online courses. You publish a regular podcast. Not only that, but you're excited about getting visible and growing your community exponentially. You love the idea of reaching new people each week.

Leadership and Outsourcing

You're a leader in your field, and you're not scared to stand out in the crowded industry that you work in. People know you as an expert, and you're consistently being invited for speaking opportunities and interviews. You don't even have to work at being visible anymore, but you do—because you love it!

As for outsourcing, you know that other people can do things better than you can—like admin and accounting. So you hire professionals who enjoy doing those things. You focus on your zone of genius, which gives you more time to step up as a leader and shine your light.

Learning

You love learning new things, and you're very discerning about what you choose to spend your time on. Which skills do you need to learn yourself, and which skills can you outsource to a professional? It's all obvious to you, and you take action accordingly. You choose to spend time only on the skills that will enhance your zone of genius and get you visible. Everything else gets outsourced.

Lifestyle

You have both a business that you love and a life that you love. Business-life balance is in harmony. You easily manage your stress levels, which gives you more time and energy to focus on raising your visibility. The more visible you are, the more comfortable life is.

Marketing and Sales

These things come easy to you because you're highly visible as a professional in your field. Prospective clients come to you regularly and consistently because your marketing is regular and consistent. You love helping them find the best package of yours to sign up for. Your visibility is paying off.

Money

More visibility means more money: more paying clients, more people buying your books and products, and more people signing up for your courses and talks. The more visible you are, the easier business is. You have a thousand raving fans who jump to buy your next product or sign up for your new service. Not only that, but you've got plenty more clients and customers who have purchased from you.

Personal Power

Visibility has led to an increased sense of personal power for you. Your self-awareness, self-trust, self-love, self-acceptance, self-esteem, self-confidence, self-respect, and self-worth have all improved exponentially. You feel great, and you're using this sense of power to help others. You're using your power for good.

Strategy, Clarity, and Vision

You have a clear vision of what you want your business and life to look like, and you have a strategy to get there. Each year, you upgrade your vision and your strategy, and each year you improve your visibility. You're growing more and more visible with each year, thanks to your efforts. Your strategy is paying off.

Success and Opportunities

The more visible you are, the more successful you feel. Opportunities come your way, and you don't have to work so hard to get them. You're invited to be a guest on someone else's podcast, which is a perfect fit. You apply to speak at a conference, and your application is accepted.

Value and Self-Worth

As you grow and as your visibility increases, your sense of value and self-worth grow also. More people know who you are now, giving you more opportunities to shine, and more opportunities to help people. The more you help others, the better you feel about yourself. And the more your business grows.

Take action today

Go through each category and write down what your dream would be for each one—what you would like to experience in terms of visibility for each category.

1. What actions would you take in your business if you were more visible? What are some bigger goals that you'd like to set for yourself?
2. How would you like to feel about change and growth? How would you like your visibility to change and grow this year?
3. What would your client relationships look like,

feel like, and sound like if you were more visible?

4. How would it be if you had a strong sense of self-confidence? What would it feel like to truly trust yourself? How would your visibility be different?
5. How would you express yourself creatively if you had bigger visibility?
6. How would you step up as a leader if you were more visible? What would that look like?
7. How would your learning habits change if you were more visible?
8. How would your lifestyle change if you were more visible with your business?
9. What would your marketing and sales practices look like if you were more visible?
10. What would your finances and your money situation look like if you were more visible? What would be different?
11. If you were more visible, what would your sense of personal power look like, feel like, and sound like?
12. If you were visible in a bigger way, what would your business strategy look like? What would your vision look like for your business?
13. What would success look like for you if you were more visible? What opportunities would you like to come your way?
14. How would you feel about your sense of value and self-worth if you were more visible?

5

CLARIFY YOUR VISION & GOALS

"Outstanding people have one thing in common: An absolute sense of mission."

— *Zig Ziglar*

We're going to start by clarifying your vision and goals because knowing exactly what you want for your business will help you uncover your specific visibility blocks. That's because you need to know what your ideal business looks like, sounds like, and feels like so you can set specific goals that will help you get there. Also, once you create an action plan to help you build your business, all sorts of mind gremlins will pop up and rear their heads. These are the blocks that you'll need to release to release your visibility blocks and build your business more quickly and easily.

Your vision

Your business vision is a clear mental image of what you want your business to be like in the future, based on your goals and dreams. Having a clear business vision will give you a clear path of action, and it can prevent you from getting off track. These days, there are many distractions in business, and it can be easy to get off course by following every bright, shiny object out there.

There are two ways you can do this: by writing out a description of what you want your business to be like, or you can go the visual route by creating a vision board—or both. I'm going to show you how to use both of these techniques to create a clear vision for your business.

What do you need to know to create a clear business vision? While different details will be important to different people, here are some of the things that will get you started thinking about what your big business vision looks like:

- How much money do you want to be making? Now stretch that goal. Stop playing small: how much money do you *really* want to be making, if anything were possible? No limits!
- Where do you want that money to be coming from? What types of products or services do you want to be offering, even if you're not currently offering them? Be creative, even if you don't think you're capable of doing those things. No limits!
- How many days do you want to be working each week? How many hours per day? Where do you want to be working? Don't worry about whether or not you think it's possible; write down what you really, really want. No limits!

- How do you want to be visible with your business? What types of things do you want to create so you can attract your ideal clients? Do you want to be a bestselling author? Do you want to have an active YouTube channel? Do you want to be an inspiring keynote speaker? How do you want to get out there in front of your ideal clients? Let yourself dream big. No limits!

Add details

How can you clarify your vision and goals? Take a look at other entrepreneurs and what their businesses look like. What elements of their business do you wish you had? What things do you wish were different for you? Take a look at what you want and write it down.

It's important to raise our awareness of as many details as we can about what we want, and it's essential to dream big. Sometimes, we can be afraid of voicing (or even just secretly writing down) our dreams because of fear. Maybe we're scared that we're not good enough to achieve these goals, or that other people will make fun of us for dreaming so big. No one needs to see what you're writing down here! Give yourself permission to dream big.

If we dream small, then we'll continue to play small. Dial up your vision for your business and make it vibrant, juicy, and exciting. The more appealing it is to you, the easier it will be for you to work toward your vision. If you've watered down your dreams, you'll end up with a vision that you don't care about, and it will be much harder to take any action toward your goals.

Trust me. Small dreams are hard to work toward. I've been there.

Was that clear? Write down your big business vision, add even more detail to it, and then dial it up. Make it more vivid, more intense, and more thrilling.

Are you having trouble dreaming big? Or maybe you just need more help with the details. I've got a free worksheet and audio download with a guided meditation that will help you get even more clarity on your big business vision. It will also help you to dial up that vision and make it even more vibrant, so you're not stuck playing small. You can get it here: http://www.hollyworton.com/111/.

Vision board

Maybe you're not a writer. Perhaps you're a very visual person who is drawn more to images. Creating a vision board can be an alternative way of expressing your big business vision, or you can create one in addition to the work you did in writing out your vision.

A vision board, also called a treasure map, is a kind of collage of images that represent your dreams for your business and life, such as the things that you want to be, do, and have. It can include inspiring words or phrases, or just pictures of what you want to experience. A vision board can be a compelling way of bringing these things into your life.

If a vision board is something you've done before, but not had much success with, I'm going to share some tips on how to make them more useful. And if you've never created one before, then I'm going to break it down into step-by-step details of what to do.

There are two main ways to create a vision board. First, we'll talk about how to create one out of magazine clipping and printed photographs and images. Then, we'll discuss how to create a digital vision board.

Top tips for a successful vision board:

1. Collect enough materials. I've got a list below to help you with that. The main thing is to have enough magazines for images. If you start with a small selection of magazines, it can make the process difficult. What I do is to collect magazines that I think might be appropriate for vision boarding throughout the year. That way, I don't have to rush around at the last minute when I feel inspired to create a new board.
2. Set aside enough time. Plan at least one hour to search through the magazines for images, at least an hour for sorting through the images you've selected, and at least 30 minutes to actually paste the images on your board. That's a minimum of two and a half hours, not including the prep work that you'll want to do (steps 3-6 below).
3. Clear your mind before starting, so you can be present and focus more easily on the process. I have what I call a "mind decluttering meditation" that might help. You can also do whatever meditation you usually practice.
4. Write a quick gratitude list of ten things you're grateful for. This helps you to take stock of what you already have. You might want to keep this focused on your business since we're doing a business vision board, but you can write down anything that you're grateful for.
5. Get clear on what you *don't* want. Don't want a business partner? Don't want to work long hours? Don't want to have to travel for business?

Don't want to see clients in person? Write it all down.

6. What would you rather have instead? Write that down. This step may help you get even more clarity toward your business vision, and it will help you focus on what you do want, not what you don't want (though the previous step is important on helping you to get clarity).
7. Go with your feelings, not with logic. This is one of the most important steps, and I'll get more into detail below.
8. Trust that your vision can come true, even if it seems impossible. Allow yourself to dream big. You'll identify and clear any blocks that may hold you back from achieving this vision after you've created the board.
9. Hang your board in a place where you can see it every day, like on the wall in behind your desk. Since this is a business vision board, it makes sense to have it in your place of work, but you can hang it anywhere that you'll see it regularly.
10. Remember what it felt like to create the board and to put all the images together. Was it excitement? A sense of thrill about what the future might bring? Tap into that feeling whenever you look at the board.
11. Express gratitude when you start being, doing, or having the things on your board. You may want to circle, highlight, or cross things off your board once they start happening. This is an important step, because it helps you to recognize the changes you've experienced in your life and the goals that you've achieved.

Collect your materials:

- Something to use as a base: you can use construction paper, cardboard, canvas, or anything else you like as a base for your vision board. I use a piece of size A3 paper.
- A variety of magazines, being sure to include at least some of the following types: travel magazines or brochures (you can get old ones for free from travel agencies...just tell them you need them for a school project, or simply ask them for old magazines); inspirational, spiritual, or personal development magazines (these often have good headlines, words, and phrases you can cut out); home and garden magazines (they might have images of nice offices, or a home you hope to purchase with income from your growing business); publications with images of people, both men and women. You can ask hairdressers and doctors' offices for their old magazines; many of them throw them out each month when the new ones arrive.
- A photograph of yourself that you like (after all, you'll be looking at this every day).
- Rubber cement, or other rubbery glue. A glue stick may work, but it can dry up and the images can fall off. It all depends on the base that you use for your board.
- Any other creative elements that you wish to use: glitter, shells, feathers, confetti, or colored paper or wrapping paper to use as a background. Whatever comes to mind.

Once you've got all your materials together, set aside enough uninterrupted time to sort through your materials and create your board: as I suggested earlier, at least two and a half hours. Clear off a large table, such as your dining table, so you have enough room to spread out your materials. Put down a tablecloth if needed to prepare the space. Sit down at the table and begin.

Board creation:

1. Clear your mind with the mind decluttering meditation I suggested earlier to get rid of anything that may distract you during the vision board process.
2. Write a quick gratitude list of ten things you're grateful for.
3. Get clear on what you don't want.
4. What would you rather have instead?
5. Now, browse through your entire stack of magazines, taking your time. Look for images that catch your attention, and for things that resonate with you. Go with your gut feeling when selecting images, rather than searching specifically for certain elements. You may be surprised at what comes up. You might want to flip quickly through the pages and stop when something catches your eye. Tear out or cut out all of the images that your intuition draws your attention to. Spend at least an hour doing this. If you find that it takes less time, go back through your magazines to see if you find anything new.
6. Sort through your images. Place your base board or

paper within reach, so you have a clear idea of the amount of space that you have. This is the time to decide which images will find their space on your board, and which ones don't make the cut. You may find it easiest to sort them into three piles: images that you definitely want on your board, images that you like least, and images that you're undecided on.

7. Put your base board or paper in front of you, and glue your photograph in the center. Gather together the images that you're certain you want on the board, and arrange them loosely over the base. Once you're happy with the arrangement, you can trim them down as needed. Then glue them into place.
8. Reflect on your finished vision board. Does anything surprise you? Does it look how you expected? What have you learned from your board? What did you learn from this process? What details has it given you about your big business vision?
9. Hang your board in a place where you can see it every day, like on the wall behind your desk.
10. Pay attention to any changes in your life that are aligned with the images on your board. The value of having a vision board in your workspace is that you can see it all day, every day. This will help you to clearly see when you start achieving some of the milestones in your vision.

The first vision board that I created using this method made no sense to me whatsoever. It was a series of nature images on a sheet of blue A4 paper: woodlands, lakes, and rivers. It was all beautiful, but it meant nothing to me. Still, I hung it up on my wall behind my desk.

Three months later, I moved out of London to a small town in the countryside that is full of fields and woods, with a river running through it. At that point, it all made sense. Some part of me was craving a more natural environment to live in.

Vision boards also work best when updated regularly. Things change, and so does your vision for your business. You can update your vision board (and your big business vision) frequently (once a year, twice a year, or quarterly) or whenever it feels appropriate.

I create a new vision board whenever I feel that I've outgrown my previous one, even if I haven't achieved everything on it. There always reaches a point where my vision board doesn't feel right anymore, and that's when I know that it's time to make a change. I always keep my current board on the wall behind my computer, and I look at it numerous times throughout the day. Even when I'm not consciously staring at it, it's always there in the background, in my field of vision.

Digital vision board

Some people prefer to create a digital vision board that they can use as their desktop wallpaper on their computer, tablet, or smartphone. Because you won't have digital magazines to flip through, this will probably be a much more logical process to creating a vision board. Search online for photographs and collect them in a folder on your computer.

Then you can use whatever photo editing software you like to create a larger image. You can use Photoshop, GIMP, or even Canva to create a digital vision board. Using this larger image as the wallpaper on your computer, tablet, or phone will help you to see the vision board regularly.

You could also create a pinboard on Pinterest with a collection of images, but this makes it more difficult for you to access the board regularly. You'll have to remember to log into Pinterest to view your pictures. There are apps you can use to create a digital vision board. If you search online, you can find a suitable solution for your board.

Your goals

Now that you've got your big business vision, start thinking of all the things you want to achieve in your business as part of that big business vision. Write down all the big and small things that occur to you: they can be a big project like writing a book or something smaller, like writing regular blog posts. Make a note of everything that comes to mind.

Focus primarily on all the things you want to achieve that will make you and your business visible so you can attract your ideal clients. What do you want to do that will help you to shine your light and help people find you? Write everything down, no matter how much it scares you.

This is so important because no matter how much mindset work we do, we still need to take practical action toward our achieving our dreams. We need to dream big, and also consider the practical steps that will take us there. It's also essential because identifying these steps will help bring up our visibility blocks.

What are goals, anyway? A goal is a desired result that a person envisions, plans, and commits to achieve. It's that simple. Etymologically speaking, the word comes from the Middle English word *gol*, meaning boundary or limit.

Goals are essential because, without them, you take a bunch of random actions. If you take enough action, things will happen, and your business will grow—but will it grow in the direction you want it to? I know plenty of people who have worked hard and expanded their business into a time-consuming monster that was so stressful to manage that they had to pause everything and go back to the drawing board.

I'm sure you can imagine that it's much easier to plan things from the start, can't you? That way, you know what you're working toward, you can make sure you're heading in the right direction, and you can have valuable milestones to mark your progress.

I started doing kickboxing in 2015, and one of the things that I like about having a belt system (white belt, red belt, etc.) is that I have regular grading days (three or four times a year), with clear things I have to achieve to progress to the next belt. I know exactly what I'm going to be graded on, and I can practice each technique before grading day.

Business is the same, except the only person who's responsible for setting goals, is *you*. Entrepreneurs make up their own rules and set their personal milestones. And if you fail to do so, there's no one else to step in and do it for you. No one is going to come along and ask you to perform a list of tasks to advance to the next business belt.

I need to clarify at this point that your vision and goals for your business absolutely can change. They're not set in stone. In fact, as you transform your mindset and grow your business, your vision and goals probably will change. That's perfectly natural.

But you have to start somewhere. Set your goals now, and then change them whenever they no longer represent the milestones you want to achieve on the path to creating your big business vision. Whenever you review your list of goals and realize that some of them don't feel right anymore, you'll know it's time to change them.

Maybe they don't feel as exciting and juicy as they did when you first set the goals. Or perhaps you've learned more about what it takes to achieve those goals, and you'd rather invest your time and energy into something else. Either way, if they no longer feel right for you, it's time for a change.

How can you set goals? The standard guideline for goal setting since the 1980s has been to create SMART goals: specific, measurable, achievable, relevant, and time-bound. There are different versions of what the letters in the acronym stand for, so you may be familiar with a slightly different explanation of what each letter stands for.

Now, I know SMART goals are a bit old school, and I even saw a Facebook ad the other day that declared the death of SMART goals, but I think they're a great place to start. If you're already clear on what SMART goals are and how to create them, go ahead and skip this section. Otherwise, let's explore SMART goal setting by using this book as an example. I knew I wanted to write a third short book in my business mindset series, and I knew I wanted to focus on visibility.

- Specific: I wanted to update and publish a book about business visibility.
- Measurable: I wanted the book to be about 40,000 words long, more or less.
- Achievable: I had already updated two other books of this length earlier in the year, so I knew it was achievable. To make sure, I booked my June "workcation weekend" to focus on updating the book and editing the final draft of the book.
- Relevant: Because visibility is one of the issues I've most struggled with and because it's one of

the most common issues that my clients bring to me, I knew it was relevant to others. Writing this book would serve two functions: it would help people to become more visible with their businesses, and it would also help me to be more visible with my other business mindset books.

- Time-bound: I wanted to release it in August 2020.

To sum it all up into one statement, as we're usually taught with SMART goals, we create a sentence that's in the present tense and which includes the elements I detailed above. So the goal would be to: *update and publish my 40,000-word* Business Visibility *book by the end of August 2020.*

Got it? It's super easy. The importance of making a goal SMART is that it encourages you to get more specific about the details. It also gives you a deadline for completion. I don't know about you, but deadlines really help me to get things done. Otherwise, projects can just go on forever.

If I hadn't made it that specific, I could have ended up with a goal such as: *Write and release a book this summer.*

Now what does that even mean? Creating such a vague goal brings up the following questions:

- Am I talking about a business book? A travel book (I also write books about my long distance walking adventures)? A fiction book?
- How long will the book be?
- Would I have to find an agent, who would then pitch the book to publishers?
- Would I be releasing a paperback or an ebook?
- When would I release it? June, July, August,

> maybe early September? Summer runs from mid-June to mid-September in the northern hemisphere. That's pretty vague.

And so many more questions, that it's not worth bringing them up. Can you see how important it is to identify concrete details about what you want to achieve before you get started? Otherwise, how do you know exactly what to do? By creating a specific goal, it helps us to not only achieve it more quickly, but it also helps us to uncover the blocks we may have that prevent us from achieving it. Later on, we'll talk more about how to identify our specific visibility blocks.

What if you're feeling so blocked that you can't think of anything? The next section should help you a little bit. If you're feeling stressed about all of this, take a break for a few minutes. Have a glass of water to rehydrate and ground yourself, and then continue when you're ready.

What if you don't achieve your goals? That's fine. That probably indicates one of two things—or both: your big business vision may have changed, meaning that your goals no longer represent a step toward achieving this vision. If this is the case, then you need to come up with new goals. It may also indicate that you've got blocks preventing you from quickly taking action toward achieving your goals. We'll discuss that in a bit.

Take action today

Go through this chapter again and get clear on your big business vision. Create a vision board for your business if it feels like something you'd like to do. Set some goals for yourself.

6

VISIBILITY BELIEFS

In my first book, *Business Beliefs*, I talk about clarifying the specific beliefs you need to achieve your big business vision. I include this list of 100 belief statements which you might find useful to help you achieve your business and visibility goals. I also tell you how to test whether or not you believe these statements at the subconscious level, how to find the priority beliefs you need to change, and what techniques and modalities to use to make these changes.

First, get clear on what a high visibility business looks like for you (revisit the last chapter). What does your big business vision look like, feel like, and sound like? How will you be visible? How will people find you?

Next, get clear on what you need to believe about yourself to make this vision a reality. Who do you need to be to get visible in a big way? What do you need to believe to be visible like Danielle Laporte, Arianna Huffington, or Oprah?

Finally, review this list of 100 belief statements about visibility. Re-word them so that they sound like your language. Highlight the ones that you'd like to believe. Then do the mindset work to reprogram these beliefs at the subconscious level (more on that later, in Chapter 14).

1. It's safe and appropriate for me to stand out and be visible.

2. I love standing out from the crowd like a tall poppy.

3. It's safe to stand out in new ways.

4. I feel comfortable being different from others.

5. I feel safe being different from other entrepreneurs.

6. It's safe and appropriate for me to be a business star.

7. I am ready to be seen both online and offline.

8. It's easy and effortless for me to claim my space in the world.

9. It's safe for me to be seen anywhere.

10. It's easy for me to share value on video.

11. My stories show people what's possible for them.

12. It's easy to make myself heard and participate in groups.

13. It's safe and comfortable for me to be visible and in the spotlight.

14. I feel confident and happy with myself when people look at me.

15. I am ready to put myself out there with my new business.

16. I am safe even if I have online haters and trolls.

17. People find it easy to find me because I am easily accessible both online and offline.

18. It's easy for me to speak up spontaneously.

19. It's safe and appropriate for me to be the center of attention.

20. I am a natural on camera and people love my videos.

21. It's safe to stand out and be an expert in my field.

22. I feel confident when filming videos and it's easy for me to watch myself on video.

23. It's okay to be out there in front of people telling my story.

24. It's safe and appropriate for me to shine online.

25. It's safe for me to shine my light out into the world.

26. I love the feeling of shining like a star.

27. I am inspired by the accomplishments of others, and others are inspired by mine.

28. I naturally find it easy to be visible, even in new situations.

29. My timing in my videos is impeccable, and I always know what to say.

30. I deeply appreciate and accept my efforts to be more visible with my business.

31. I am proud of how my visibility has increased both online and offline.

32. I accept my imperfections in my writing and my videos.

33. It's easy for me to create inspiring, popular videos.

34. I allow myself to be vulnerable in my writing and my videos.

35. It's easy for me to express my uniqueness online.

36. I have a large audience which listens to what I have to say.

37. It's safe and appropriate for me to be me and to express who I am.

38. It's my purpose to show up in the world and share my story.

39. I am seen and valued for my expertise.

40. I'm seen and acknowledged for my achievements.

41. It's my time to be in the spotlight, and I'm ready for it.

42. My audience is ready for me to put this out in a big way.

43. I inspire people all over the world with my work.

44. I am a big business celebrity with a raving tribe of fans.

45. I speak with clarity and strength.

46. I shine my light out into the world and attract my ideal clients.

47. I have a thriving online tribe of people who jump to buy my things.

48. I'm fully comfortable in the spotlight.

49. I'm ready, willing, and able to receive judgement.

50. I love pitching myself for PR and media opportunities because it gets me clients.

51. I love being visible with my business.

52. I enjoy publicly celebrating my accomplishments.

53. It's easy for me to share my accomplishments with others.

54. It's easy for me to speak up and ask questions.

55. I express myself fully in a loving way.

56. I easily bring out those things that are most profound inside me.

57. It's easy for me to outwardly express and externalize my divinity.

58. I'm safe when I'm tall and elevated.

59. I'm safe when I ascend to a high space.

60. I am here to be big and visible.

61. My divine mission is to help people on a global level.

62. I stand out energetically in a very big way.

63. My destiny is to stand out globally.

64. People want to hear what I have to say.

65. I own my presence on a big stage.

66. I claim my space on the big stage.

67. I expand my vision globally.

68. I embody all of who I am when I am on stage.

69. I'm a great podcast guest that everyone wants to interview.

70. It's easy for me to be accepted as a guest on other podcasts.

71. People love it when I show up as my unique self.

72. It's safe and appropriate for people to disagree with me.

73. It's safe and appropriate for people to criticize me.

74. It's safe and appropriate for me to speak my truth.

75. It's safe and appropriate for me to be powerful and known.

76. I have a steady stream of media outlets approaching me.

77. The media sees me as an expert in [your field of expertise].

78. I am famous for [your field of expertise].

79. I am THE go-to person for [your field of expertise].

80. I clearly express myself openly.

81. People flock to hear me, see me, and be in my tribe.

82. It's safe and appropriate for me to be different.

83. I easily radiate my gifts out to the world.

84. I give myself permission to share my gifts far and wide.

85. I easily speak up and express myself fully.

86. I share my message in a way that's aligned with my higher self.

87. It's safe and appropriate for me to share what I know with the world.

88.I easily radiate my brilliance as a messenger of truth.

89. It's safe and appropriate for me to reveal the brilliance of my light.

90. I easily easily show up in the fullest expression of myself.

91. I easily allow myself to take up space to shine.

92. The more I shine my light, the more I connect with others.

93. It's easy for me to radiate brilliance and vulnerability.

94. It's easy for me to connect with my audience and expand my reach.

95. I am loved, noticed, and appreciated.

96. I am ready, willing, and able to be seen.

97. I am ready, willing, and able to take up space.

98. I am ready, willing, and able to appear regularly in people's timelines.

99. It's easy for me to build a thriving community, both online and offline.

100. Speaking opportunities come to me easily and regularly.

Take action today

Go through this list and highlight the beliefs you think would be most useful to you. If you have my book *Business Beliefs*, re-read Chapter 9, which talks about how to self-muscle test each belief to see which ones you hold at the subconscious level. You can also muscle test to identify the highest priority beliefs for you to change.

7

VISIBILITY BLOCKS

"Cultivate visibility because attention is currency."

— Chris Brogan

I talk a lot about blocks in my second book, *Business Blocks: Transform Your Self-Sabotaging Mind Gremlins, Awaken Your Inner Mentor, and Allow Your Business Brilliance to Shine*. There's even a section on visibility blocks in that book. But because visibility has been such a big issue for me personally and for my clients, I thought it was essential to write a separate book specifically on this topic.

A visibility block is anything that stops us from being more visible with our business, whether online or offline. It could refer to any fears, blocks, limiting beliefs, or self-doubt that is triggered when we think about making ourselves more visible with our business via marketing, networking, and sales. It's the thing that leads us to procrastinate and avoid doing what we need to do to be seen by our ideal clients. It's anything that disrupts or negatively affects the degree to which the public sees our businesses.

Visibility blocks are the mind gremlins that hold you back from taking action to make yourself more visible with your business. Or perhaps you take action, and then sabotage yourself in some other way, making it feel like you're taking one step forward and one step backward in your business. They're what keep you feeling stuck and frustrated with your business—like you've hit a plateau or invisible ceiling.

They can show up in so many ways: fears of online trolls and "haters," impostor syndrome (fear of being found out to be a fraud), fears of criticism. So many things can come up when we stretch outside of our comfort zone and put ourselves out there in a more significant way because we open ourselves up to a much wider audience...and that bigger audience isn't always kind.

Visibility, as I've said, was a *massive* issue for many of my clients, which is not a surprise, considering that visibility was a big issue for me to overcome. Visibility blocks can show up in many ways: fears of online trolls and "haters", impostor syndrome (fear of being found out to be a fraud), and fears of criticism. So many things can come up when we stretch outside of our comfort zone and put ourselves out there in a more significant way because we open ourselves up to a much wider audience—and that bigger audience isn't always kind.

When you're marketing your business, whether it's online or offline, you need to be visible. Otherwise, you end up being the best-kept secret in your field. Increasing your visibility means being willing to be seen and being willing to take up space, two elements that my fabulous business coach/mentor Lisa Wechtenhiser (www.lisamw.com) introduced me to via work that she's done with Fabeku Fatunmise (www.fabeku.com).

As I mentioned earlier, the rebranding I did in early 2016 triggered a lot of stuff for me, and I was only able to follow through with the rebrand as a result of all the mindset upgrading I had done. But still: my face was all over my website, as was my name. My face was on my Facebook cover photo and my new podcast artwork. It was everywhere. It scared the crap out of me. I was making myself super visible. I was more willing to be seen than ever before, but it was still a stretch outside of my comfort zone.

Being willing to take up space could mean physically (standing up on a stage and speaking) or virtually (showing up in people's Facebook timelines and YouTube subscriptions and inbox emails). This is *the* big issue for me: for years, I promised email subscribers that I'd never email them more than once a month because I didn't want to take up space in their inbox. I didn't post too much on Facebook because I didn't want to take up space on their timeline. I remember a time when I posted two videos on YouTube and the same two videos on Facebook, and I felt sick. How dare I take up two videos' worth of space on someone's timeline??!!

Does any of this ring a bell for you? These are what visibility blocks look like. I've done loads of work on mine, and it's finally paying off. Some of the things that I do are still a stretch outside my comfort zone, but it's easier for me to take the actions.

Symptoms of blocks

Here's a more detailed explanation of symptoms that you may be struggling with blocks in the area of Visibility. Be sure to make note of which ones you're currently experiencing in your business. And if you haven't already, go back to Chapter 3 and highlight the symptoms of low visibility that you resonate with.

Do any of these sound familiar? If so, make note of them in your journal so that you can later do the work to release these blocks.

- You want to build your email list, and you've heard that a great way to do that would be to set up Facebook ads to drive traffic to your opt-in offers, but it freaks you out to think of your ads showing up in the news feeds of all those people they don't know.
- You'd love to build a YouTube channel for my business, but you hate how you look and sound on video. Plus, comments on YouTube videos can be horrendous. How could you deal with reading all those horrible things people might say about you?
- You're afraid of participating in Facebook groups; you'd like people to get to know what you do, but you're so scared of saying the wrong thing that you lurk in silence and read what everyone else has to say.
- You write regular blog posts, but you never promote them online. You're afraid of getting nasty comments on your posts...even though you could delete them if they were just trolls. The thought of getting negative comments on your writing makes your stomach churn.
- You'd like to start doing webinars, but you just can't seem to get started. You've tried putting the slides together and you just keep getting stuck every time. You feel like you'll never manage to get your first webinar out there.

Discover your blocks

Here are a few questions to help you get clear on your business blocks:

- What's really stopping you from setting up those Facebook ads (or Amazon Ads, or something else)?
- What's the worst that could happen if unknown people saw them? What might they say or do to you?
- Are you afraid of getting negative comments or reviews? Are you scared of haters? Are you worried people will say bad things about you?
- What kinds of negative things are you afraid of people saying? What's the worst thing that someone could say about you?
- What's wrong with how you look and sound on video (or audio)? Are you unhappy with your appearance, or by how articulate you are? Or is it something else?
- Are you afraid that people will dislike what you have to say in your videos, on your podcast, or on your blog?
- Do you worry they'll think what you have to say isn't valid? That you don't know what you're talking about? That you aren't good enough?
- Are you scared people will laugh at you? What are you afraid they'll make fun of you for?
- What's so scary about Facebook groups, posting YouTube videos, or whatever it is that you're avoiding? What does this trigger for you?
- Perhaps you've spent hours lurking in an online community, but you haven't posted anything yet.

If you've spent enough time in the group to know the dynamics and the individuals in there, what's stopping you from speaking up and participating? What do you think people will say or think about you? Are you afraid of posting something inappropriate? What's the worst that could happen?

- What's stopping you from promoting your blog/videos/podcast/books to a wider audience? Are you afraid that people will think you don't know what you're talking about? That your message is too basic? That you're not good enough?
- What's going on with your webinars, or anything else that you've been avoiding, like teaching an online course? Are you afraid that people will attend your trainings and think you're a fraud? That they'll call you out on how little you know? That you'll be caught without an answer? That they'll say you don't know enough to run a business around what you do?
- What's the worst that could happen if you ran a webinar, online course, or other event and opened yourself up to people's feedback?

Examples of blocks

Sometimes it can be hard to identify our blocks, especially if we're just getting started digging them up. Here are some examples that might help you to identify your business blocks or limiting beliefs in the area of Visibility:

- It's scary to put myself out there in a bigger way.

- I hate the thought of getting online haters and trolls; I could never deal with that.
- I'm afraid of people criticizing my work.
- I'm not good enough to seek out a speaking engagement.

As I mentioned earlier, it's often easier to spot the symptoms of visibility blocks than to see the blocks themselves, which we often have to dig deeper to find. Anytime we're not making as much money as we like, or struggle to bring in enough clients, this is often a result of visibility blocks.

We often talk about playing small, and this is another visibility block. If you have ever felt like you downplayed your success with a client, or in your business, so that you didn't stand out and look amazing, this is a visibility block. If you ever held back from celebrating your business successes with the important people in your life, this is a visibility block.

If you think of your business as an island, with you as the lighthouse on the island, shining your light out there to let people know where you are, how does that feel? If you envision yourself beaming out your energy to attract your ideal clients to you, does that feel anything less than fantastic? If so, you may be experiencing visibility blocks.

I want to help you shine your light into the world, so your ideal clients can find you and work with you. You're not helping anyone by dimming your light and playing small. On the contrary, you're preventing your ideal clients from finding you. You're doing them a disservice by not allowing them to be helped by you.

When you release your visibility blocks, you'll more easily attract clients. Your ideal clients will sign up to work with *you*, rather than going with their second-best option—

because they've heard of you and have had a chance to get to know your work online. You'll spend less time and effort marketing your business because everything will be easier to take action on. All of this means that your business will be making money consistently: you'll trade feast or famine for a steady stream of clients.

Don't you think it's time to release your visibility blocks and stop playing small? Let's get started.

Take action today

Go through this chapter again and write down any visibility blocks that you're currently experiencing. It's important to know exactly where you stand today so that you can do the work to transform your mindset.

8

IDENTIFY YOUR VISIBILITY BLOCKS

"We need to accept that we won't always make the right decisions, that we'll screw up royally sometimes – understanding that failure is not the opposite of success, it's part of success."

— ARIANNA HUFFINGTON

We must become aware of what our visibility blocks are because it's the first step in transforming our blocks into enhancing beliefs that will help you create the business of our dreams. You can't release those blocks if you don't know what they are. Clarity is powerful.

We've already talked a little about what visibility blocks are. They are anything that stops us from being able to be more visible with our business, whether it's online or offline. They are any fears, blocks, limiting beliefs, or self-doubt that is triggered when we think about making ourselves more visible with our business with marketing, networking, and sales.

How can you become aware of your visibility blocks? It's easy once you get started. The more you become aware of your blocks, the easier it will be to spot them. I recommend keeping a notebook, a journal, or a document on your computer where you can make a note of all your blocks, so you can later work on them.

There are eight main ways to uncover and identify your specific visibility blocks, and it's worth exploring your blocks from all different aspects. I'm going to list the eight ways here, and then delve deeper into each one, so you understand how they work.

Here they are, in no particular order:

1. Reading books
2. Exploring your fears
3. Looking at triggers from your Big Business Vision
4. Discovering triggers from coaching/mentoring
5. Looking at how you procrastinate
6. Recording day to day blocks
7. Taking action
8. Digging even deeper

Reading books

Whenever I read a book, I pay attention to any fears, blocks, or limiting beliefs that come up. Awareness is the first step, and I've trained my brain to perk up when I read a passage that indicates an area where I might have a block. I never read a business book without keeping in mind the opportunity to uncover new blocks.

If I'm reading a paperback, I underline each passage

that triggers my awareness of a block, and if I'm reading an ebook, I highlight each passage, then copy and paste it into an email to myself. This is how I record the bits of the book that have helped me to uncover new blocks.

From there, I add these new blocks into my system by adding them to my notebook of things to work on in my next PSYCH-K® session, either with myself or with another facilitator. If I was reading a paperback, I make a note of the book title, so I remember to go through the underlined passages. If I was reading an ebook, I wait until I've finished the book, and I combine all of my notes into one Word document, which I then print out and add to my notebook.

Start with this book. Make a note of any business blocks that you uncover as you read. Go through my other two business books and note any other blocks that come up for you.

Whenever you read a business or marketing book, be alert for any visibility blocks that you may become aware of based on the material you read. Regular books are a gold mine to help you uncover blocks.

Not long before writing the first edition of this book, I read Michelle Lowbridge's book *Wealthology: The Science of Smashing Money Blocks*. It helped me to identify new money blocks that I hadn't previously been aware of. I copied and pasted the passages from the ebook that applied to me, then printed them out and created belief statements based on the material. Finally, I used PSYCH-K® to balance those beliefs by programming them into my subconscious.

Michelle's book is short and actionable, and I made great use of it by taking all the bits that applied to me and using them to upgrade my mindset.

Exploring your fears

What things are you afraid of in business? Are you afraid of public speaking, sales conversations, networking, or something else? I include a big list of possible triggers in Chapter 10, where I talk about marketing and sales, so it may help you to go through those and make a note of what fears you have.

From that list, I can tell you that I had huge fears around Facebook advertising. I was afraid of overwhelming people by showing up too often on their timeline with my ads. I was scared of tweeting too much; that people would get sick of seeing me in their Twitter feed. Rationally, I knew that most entrepreneurs follow so many people that they're unlikely to be bombarded with my messages. But I had to clear the blocks to enable me to be more visible on social media.

I had fears around email newsletters. I tend to get overwhelmed by people who email too much, and so I promised never to email people more than once a month, even though I knew that wasn't enough to be effective. Once I realized that was a visibility block, I had to do the work to transform those beliefs and allow myself to send more frequent emails to my list.

Discovery calls were also a source of fear for me. I would freak out when unknown people signed up for a discovery call. If I had never heard of the person before, it made me nervous about the call. This was all about being seen one-to-one by someone new. I released the blocks, and discovery calls became fun.

Video is a significant source of visibility blocks for many of my clients. Creating videos can be a great way of connecting with people, but it can also be terrifying. Once you identify exactly why you're afraid of video (or other forms of content), it can make it easier for you to create a thriving YouTube channel that regularly attracts new clients into your business.

Look at other entrepreneurs and what they're doing. Does any of that scare you? Maybe having a popular YouTube channel or speaking on a stage to a big audience? Sometimes, it helps us become aware of our fears by looking at other people who are further along with their businesses.

What about fear of haters, trolls, and online criticism? So many people are afraid to put their content up online because they don't want to put themselves in a position where they might receive hateful feedback. Is this an issue for you? Are you afraid of comments on your blog posts and YouTube videos? Are you afraid of truly being yourself online and being attacked for it?

Fear of rejection is a related issue. Are you afraid of potential clients saying no to you in a sales conversation? Are you so scared that people will unsubscribe if you send out a newsletter that you don't email your list at all? What other ways might people reject you? How do you feel about that?

Finally, think about what's the worst that could happen if you put yourself out there with your business. Try to imagine a worst-case scenario for being visible. It's essential to clear any fears you might have because they're probably blocking your business visibility.

Write all of these fears down in whatever system you've set up to track your visibility blocks, so you can work on them with yourself or with whatever practitioner you've chosen.

Looking at triggers from your Big Business Vision

Go back to that Big Business Vision that you created in the "Clarify Your Vision & Goals" chapter. If you haven't already done so, download my guided visualization and worksheet here: http://www.hollyworton.com/111/. Dial up that vision and make it big and juicy.

Now, look at any actions that you need to take to achieve this vision. What visibility blocks come up as a result of reviewing these actions? Are there any fears that come up for you?

Perhaps you have specific blocks around the different actions you need to take, or you may have a massive block around achieving that Big Business Vision. Do you think you're not worthy of having all that? Are you not good enough? Smart enough? These are all things that can prevent you from making yourself visible enough to achieve that big goal.

One of my big goals for my business vision was to be an author. That was so scary! Who was I to write books? Who was I to publish my work? Was I even good enough? What if people bought my books and hated them, and I got terrible reviews online? The horror!

But by not writing my books, I was playing small and dimming my light. I did the work to overcome my literary fears and blocks, and I released six books in 2016. This was my fourth, and I published two other books later that year. I see each new book as a way to turn up the light I shine out into the world with my business.

Note that I still have fears, but they're no longer paralyzing me. I'm taking action. And I'm writing books more easily and effortlessly that I ever imagined I could.

Dig deep to bring any visibility blocks to light. It's essential to become aware of as many blocks as you can.

Remember, it's super easy to transform these blocks and release them, so it doesn't matter how many you have. The more you uncover, the faster you can grow your business.

Write the visibility blocks down in the system you've set up to track your visibility blocks, so you can work on them with yourself or with whatever practitioner you've chosen. Then do the work to transform your blocks into opportunities.

Discovering triggers from coaching/mentoring

This is a big one for me. Ever since I first trained in PSYCH-K®, I've taken advantage of my business coaching and mentoring to bring to light my visibility blocks. Mentoring is perfect for this because most business coaching or mentoring sessions end with an action plan of business tasks that you agree to that will help you achieve your business goals. And often, these tasks are located outside your comfort zone.

Years ago, when I was in the middle of a coaching program with Natalie Sisson, I agreed to approach a few business friends about doing a joint venture with them to promote my online course in social media. I knew it was the next logical step to getting my program out there, but it terrified me. And so I did the mindset work to release the blocks, which made it easier to get in touch with people and propose a joint venture.

And every time I have a session with my current coach/mentor, Lisa Wechtenhiser, I end up with a list of things to do, including practical business actions and mindset stuff to upgrade. It makes them doubly useful when you become aware of the visibility blocks that your coaching sessions trigger.

Whenever you have a session with your business coach

or mentor, write down any blocks that come up in whatever system you've set up to track your visibility blocks so that you can work on them with yourself or with your chosen practitioner.

Looking at how you procrastinate

I'm good at hyper-focusing to get work done, but I also procrastinate. Whenever I become aware that I'm procrastinating on something, I take action right away to release the stress on whatever task I'm avoiding. PSYCH-K® has a super quick (2-5 minutes) balance to transform and release trauma and stress around any situation, past, present, or future. It's perfect for releasing stress around a dreaded task that I struggle to complete, and I use it all the time both with myself and with clients.

The alternative is to struggle on and trudge through getting the task done. But why do things the hard way, when you can make getting things done easy and effortless? I'm not a fan of "hard work" and struggle. I believe it takes work to build a business, but it doesn't necessarily have to be hard.

Brian Tracy wrote a well-known book called *Eat That Frog!*, which talks about how to conquer procrastination by getting the big tasks done first thing in the day. I think that's a fantastic way to get things done. But why not make eating those frogs even easier—and more palatable—by releasing your blocks around them first? Why suffer when you can enjoy eating frogs (or kale, if you're not a meat-eater). Doing the mindset work to release your visibility blocks is all about making business easier.

Once you become aware of all the things you're procrastinating on, write them down in whatever system you've set up to track your visibility blocks, so you can work on them with yourself or with whatever practitioner you've chosen. For this purpose of overcoming procrastination, it's ideal to have a technique that you can use with yourself, so you can blast through the procrastination blocks and get things done.

Recording day to day blocks

This is one of the most powerful ways for me to uncover my blocks. As I'm going about my day-to-day work, I've trained my mind to become aware of blocks as they arise. Once I've become aware of them, I record them in my notebook.

When I first trained in PSYCH-K®, this is how I came up with the ten to twenty blocks that I released each day. I'd write them down in my notebook, and then create belief statements to transform at the end of my workday. This simple process was hugely transformational for me, and it allowed me to quickly and easily upgrade my business mindset by releasing my blocks.

When you identify visibility blocks throughout the day, write them down in whatever system you've set up to track your visibility blocks so that you can work on them with yourself or with your chosen practitioner.

Taking action

Taking action can be a very effective way to uncover your visibility blocks. You may not realize you have blocks in a particular area until you start to take action toward a goal. Let's go back to my goal of becoming an author and writing and self-publishing books.

I set the goal of writing short, actionable books that were around 20,000 words in length. But I didn't know until I started writing that I'd be afraid that people would think they were worthless because they were too short. They're short *on purpose*, yet I was scared of putting them out there for the world to see and then getting criticism on their length.

Recently, my business coach/mentor suggested that I reach out to a handful of people on my list and invite them to have a discovery call with me, so we could get to know each other better. I had a bit of a wobble but agreed that it was a good idea. I did want to have more individual contact with the people on my list.

It wasn't until I sat down to write an individual email to each of these people that I realized what a huge block I had around being visible to each individual person. It suddenly became so much more of a thing to send ten personalized emails out than it is to send one huge email to all the people on my list. I have no idea what that's about, but I can guarantee you it makes sense to my subconscious.

Digging even deeper

It also helps to go within and look beyond the symptoms of visibility issues to examine the underlying causes of those fears, blocks, and limiting beliefs. Do you have any past trauma around being visible that needs to be released? Are you aware of anything from earlier in your life that may be blocking you from being visible now?

If you've had previous businesses that perhaps didn't go as well as you may have liked, you might have blocks and limiting beliefs around that experience. I had a lot of blocks relating to my first business that I needed to clear. There were a lot of decisions that were made by my business partner that I didn't feel good about, and this led me to develop all kinds of business blocks about not being worthy of having a successful business due to my experience. That meant that I didn't take the actions I needed to take to be more visible. I had to do so much work to clear out my past business trauma and allow myself to be more visible with my business.

Another deep core belief that many entrepreneurs struggle with is the belief that they're not good enough, which of course, affects their business visibility. If you're not happy with yourself, why would you want to be more visible? These types of beliefs can be painful to explore, but they're worth taking a look at. Plus, if you've found a way to transform your beliefs (such as with PSYCH-K® or another technique), it's fast and easy to change any painful beliefs about not feeling like you're good enough.

Let's go even deeper. Would you say that you love yourself? If you don't believe this at the subconscious level (and you can use muscle testing to figure this out; check out my first book, *Business Beliefs* to learn how), this can affect your business visibility. If you don't love yourself and think you're fantastic as a person, then it can be hard to put yourself out there with your business.

Do you believe that you deserve to have a successful business? If not, then that can be a huge visibility block. Remember, what you believe at the subconscious level may or may not be consistent with what you believe at the conscious level. So may think you believe that you deserve to have a successful business, but we need to check in with your subconscious to see what it thinks.

I've had to do a lot of work around deserving to be successful with my business, in part due to some of my experiences in my first company. I had a lot of limiting beliefs that were not serving me, which affected my business visibility. By clearing these beliefs, I was able to take action to become more visible with my business.

I hope these eight methods of uncovering visibility

blocks have been helpful for you. Everyone will have their preferred method of bringing blocks to the light, but you may find it useful to try each of the eight methods so you can see which ones work best for you. Or you may decide to use all of them.

What if you're still struggling to identify your visibility blocks? If you're feeling stressed about all of this, sit in the Whole Brain Posture for a few minutes. Have a glass of water to rehydrate and ground yourself, and then continue when you're ready.

Honestly, I can't imagine that it would be impossible for you to uncover any visibility blocks if you've tried all of these methods, but maybe you're so blocked that you can't see the blocks. In that case, go straight to working on releasing your blocks to uncovering your visibility blocks with a practitioner. Programming beliefs into your subconscious, such as "I easily become aware of my visibility blocks and work to transform them," can help you to become more aware of your blocks.

Take action today

Go through this chapter again and create a system that works for you to identify and record your blocks on a daily and weekly basis.

9

VISIBILITY FEARS

> "...my fear wants me to be safe, and my fear perceives all motion, all inspiration, all work, all activity, all passion whatsoever as potentially life-threatening. My fear wants me to live a smaller life. The smallest imaginable life, ideally. My fear would prefer that I never got out of bed."
>
> — ELIZABETH GILBERT

What is fear? It's an unpleasant and uncomfortable emotion caused by the perceived threat of danger, pain, or harm. It's a very natural emotion, and fear can be critical to our survival. Fear can be useful to us, and it can also hinder our growth and development...if we allow it to do so. There are two main types of fear: rational fear (we're out on a hike, and as we come around a bend we see a bear) and irrational fear (we avoid making a decision in our business because we're afraid we'll end up bankrupt and homeless). The first example is a situation when we're facing real-life danger, and the second is a perceived fear that may or may not occur. These perceived threats or fears are just another type of business block.

Fear usually causes us to react in one of four main ways: fight, flight, freeze, and fawn. However, we can also respond with a combination of these patterns. We may react in one way to one type of fear or conflict, and we may respond in a completely different way in another kind of situation.

Fight

This is pretty self-explanatory: it means that we respond by aggressively confronting the threat. In this type of reaction, we may feel tense, our jaw tight, our teeth clenched. We may feel intense anger like we want to punch or kick someone or something. We may even cry.

An entrepreneur who tends to fight may bully their business partner or their employees. They may attempt to damage the reputation of the other person or blame someone else to "win" the conflict. If an employee attempts to quit their job and leave the company, a fight-inclined business owner may try to coerce them into staying. Or the entrepreneur may attack a particular project and its supporters or the team involved—to the extent that they may even sabotage the project.

Flight

The exact opposite response: it means that we run away from the threat. We may feel restless and fidgety, even though we don't physically run away. We may feel trapped and tense, ready for takeoff.

A business owner who tends flight may ignore any conflict that occurs—or, worse, they may disappear altogether, not answering emails, phone calls, or other communication. In going radio silent, they avoid the situation entirely. Or they may remain present in the office, busying themselves with unimportant admin work so they can avoid the situation without anyone noticing.

Freeze

In this scenario, we find ourselves unable to fight or flight. We seem to have lost the ability to move or act in response to the threat. We may feel numb, though our heart is pounding. We may feel a sense of dread.

An entrepreneur who tends to freeze is the kind of person who does nothing in the face of fear. This is a passive response to conflict. They may, for example, avoid innovation in their field because they want to wait and see how things will turn out in their industry before taking action.

Fawn

The least well-known of the four, this response is often referred to as "people-pleasing." It's when we comply with the threatening person or accommodate their needs to save ourselves, and it's a typical response in abusive relationships. In fact, "fawn" is a term that was coined by Pete Walker, a C-PTSD (complex post-traumatic stress disorder) survivor and licensed therapist who specializes in helping adults who experienced childhood trauma.

Business owners who tend to fawn may be big people pleasers who struggle in their relationships with clients. They may avoid setting and upholding boundaries. They may feel taken advantage of by their business partner because they say "yes" to every request and suggestion that their partner makes, even if they don't agree with them. They want to avoid conflict.

Uncovering our fears

Fear is uncomfortable. Some people tend to sweep their fears under the rug, so they don't have to look at them. Unfortunately, even though the fears have been suppressed and hidden, they haven't gone away, and they're still operating in the background, affecting the person's actions and decisions.

That's why it's so important to take a look at our fears. They're just as easy to transform as other types of business blocks, but we can't do the work to release our fears until we identify what they are. There's nothing wrong or shameful about having visibility-related fears; we all have them.

Common fears

Here are some common fears relating to visibility:

- Fear of standing out in the crowd
- Fear of being seen
- Fear of getting too much attention
- Fear of criticism and negative comments
- Fear of being "canceled"
- Fear of a modern-day "witch hunt"
- Fear of expressing yourself fully
- Fear of voicing your opinions
- Fear of people finding you and stalking you

As I said earlier in this chapter, some fears are rational, some are not. When we speak up and voice our opinions online, we do open ourselves up to criticism from other people—someone of whom may react with excessive harshness. But rarely do people get famous from one day to the next, which means that most of us will have time to grow little by little, and deal with the challenges that come from upleveling our visibility.

If your dreams involve getting really big, you might want to read an excellent blog post by Tim Ferriss titled 11 Reasons Not to Become Famous (or "A Few Lessons Learned Since 2007"). It shares some of the challenges he's had in life as a result of his popularity among readers and fans, and it may give you some ideas about practical tactics you can put into place to keep yourself safe.

Take action today

Write down all the visibility fears that come to mind. Really dig deep and allow yourself to explore what's the worst that could happen if you got visible in a big way. This isn't about creating new fears, but getting clear on the ones you already hold. Remember, you're going to do the work to release these fears later on.

On the podcast

You can find the full list of podcast episodes here: www.hollyworton.com/podcast

- 331 Facing Your Fears & Overcoming Them (now with downloadable transcript!)
- 259 Jo Casey + Holly ~ What Will They Think of Me? Will They Like Me? (How to Get Past These Fears) (now with downloadable transcript!)

- 246 Jo Casey + Holly ~ How to Tell if You're Out of Alignment or Deep in Fear With Your Business (now with downloadable transcript!)
- 201 Holly Worton & 4 "Woo" Experts: How to Get Over Your Fear of Sharing Your Woo (now with downloadable transcript!)
- 137 How to Stop Hiding & Overcome Your Fear of Visibility (now with downloadable transcript!)
- 110 How to Overcome Your Business Fears
- 67 How to Overcome Fear of Not Being Good Enough, with Ann Brown

10

THE PRACTICAL SIDE OF VISIBILITY

> "I always did something I was a little not ready to do. I think that's how you grow. When there's that moment of 'Wow, I'm not really sure I can do this,' and you push through those moments, that's when you have a breakthrough."
>
> — Marissa Mayer

Now that you've clarified your vision and goals, it's time to look at the practical things you'll need to do so you can make your big business vision become a reality. Why? Because achieving your goals and fulfilling your vision means taking practical action and doing the relevant mindset work. And sometimes, looking at the action plan can help us identify our visibility blocks.

As I've said before, my first business gave me all of my practical business and online marketing knowledge, so when I started as a solopreneur with my other business, I had all the practical skills I needed. Yet I still struggled to take action on all of the things I knew I needed to do because deep down, I was terrified of being visible with my business. This held me back for years and forced me to move ahead at a snail's pace.

The practical side of visibility involves all the ways you want to be seen in your business, including how you plan to market your business—both online and offline—and what your sales process you will use to take on new clients. We're going to talk a little bit about some of the practical ways you can increase your visibility in your business, and as you read, I'd like to ask you to make a note of any fears, blocks, or limiting beliefs that come up for you as you read each section.

This is important because the whole point of this book is to help you get clarity by uncovering your blocks and bringing them to light. If I haven't yet made this clear, you'll need to take action to get results from reading this book.

Look for thoughts like:

- I could never do that because ________.
- I'm not good enough to do ________.
- What will people think if I ________?
- Doing ________ scares the crap out of me.
- I'm not ready to do ________ just yet. Maybe next year.

Also look for what one of my clients calls "yeah buts." These are the excuses that pop up into your mind when you start thinking about taking actions that will lead you outside of your comfort zone.

Here are some examples:

- If you think about going to a new networking group: "Yeah, but what if no one likes me and I end up standing all alone in the corner by myself?"
- If you consider starting a YouTube channel for your business: "Yeah, but people make horrible comments on YouTube videos and I don't want that."
- If you sign up for a Facebook ads course: "Yeah, but what if people get tired of seeing me in their timeline every day and they block me?"

Let's explore business visibility from both online and offline perspectives. Some aspects of business visibility have to do with an online presence: social media marketing and advertising, creating online content (such as a blog, podcasts, email newsletters, and videos), and the more technical aspects such as SEO (search engine optimization), which helps your website become more visible online.

Offline visibility includes networking, speaking at events, and going to trade shows or conferences. Offline marketing usually involves meeting with people face to face at some type of event, though it could include things like radio interviews. You could also send out direct mail about your business or have someone go door to door handing out flyers for you if this kind of marketing makes sense for your business.

When you look at these two main classifications of visibility (online and offline), which sounds more natural to you? Which seems more difficult? Does one type of visibility sound scarier than the other? Which one brings up more "yeah buts" for you? Write it all down.

When we have a lot of fears, blocks, and limiting beliefs around visibility, online marketing can sometimes feel safer: we're sitting at home in the comfort of our office, marketing away—but we've reached a time where so many solopreneurs have online businesses that our online audience is massive. The sheer amount of people who might see our message online can sometimes make online marketing even scarier than offline marketing. With offline marketing efforts, you're usually limited to the number of people you can see in the room, which may seem more comfortable for some people. Plus, it's easier to gauge people's reactions.

We're going to take a look now at a variety of different ways you can be visible, both online and offline. Please get out your journal or open up a new file on your computer so you can make a note of any fears, blocks, or limiting beliefs that come up for you as you read through each type of activity that can contribute to the increased invisibility of your business. I've divided these actions into two categories: marketing and sales.

Marketing

Marketing is all about communicating to others what it is that you do and how you help your clients. It's spreading the word about your business and making it visible to others.

- Advertising: online using Google AdWords, advertising on relevant websites, or advertising in local newspapers or magazines.
- Blogging: writing regular blog posts related to

your business, such as who you are, what you do, and how you help people.

- Email newsletters: writing regular emails to the people on your list to deliver valuable information, connect with them, and allow them to get to know who you are and how you might help them.
- Networking: whether you go to BNI (Business Networking International), mixed networking groups, women-only groups, or speed networking, these types of meetings can be a great way of meeting new people and letting them know what you do.
- Press releases: sending out press releases to the media when something newsworthy happens in your business, with the intention of a media outlet writing a story about you or your business.
- SEO (search engine optimization) for your website: optimizing your website so that it's more likely to show up in search results when someone searches for what you do.
- Social media marketing: using Facebook, Twitter, Pinterest, Instagram, YouTube, Periscope, LinkedIn and other social networks to network, market, and advertise your business online.
- Speaking: you can speak at networking groups, conferences, or other types of events. This helps showcase you as an expert in your field.
- Website: I tend to assume that most business owners have a website, but of course not everyone does, especially if you're just getting started in your business. A website is a great way

for potential clients to check you out online before actually getting in touch with you.
- Writing: whether it's writing guest blog posts, writing a book (like this one), or writing articles for a local newspaper or magazine, this can be a great way to showcase who you are and what you do.
- Video: creating short videos that deliver useful content and help your potential clients get a feel for whether you're a good fit for them to work with.

Sales

- Cold calling: I'm not honestly sure how much this is actually done these days, especially for the types of businesses that solopreneurs usually have, but this involves making phone calls to potential clients, then engaging them in a conversation about what it is that you do and how you might be able to help them.
- Discovery calls: inviting a person onto a call that will allow the two of you to see if you're a good fit to work together, then inviting them onto your program if you'd like to work with them.
- Speaking at events: giving an engaging talk where you share useful information, and then make an offer at the end for people to work with you.
- Webinars: getting a group of people together online to share valuable information, then making an offer at the end to encourage people to sign up to work with you.

- Workshops: delivering a workshop on one of the more basic topics you help people with, then offering an upsell to a more advanced program at the end of the event.

After looking through these lists, which of these activities sounds like a fun way to increase the visibility of your business? Which ones seem appealing, but too scary to try? Which ones make you feel sick to your stomach if you envision yourself doing them? Which ones generate one or more "yeah buts" for you? Write it all down.

Which ones do you think will help you achieve your business goals the fastest? Are these actions the scariest ones, or the easiest ones? How does it feel when you imagine taking action in these areas to increase your visibility?

Going through each of these categories should have helped you to generate a list of visibility blocks that are stopping you from getting you and your business out there in front of your ideal clients. But what if you didn't come up with anything? Trust me. The blocks are there. Even entrepreneurs who are wildly successful have mindset blocks: new ones simply pop up as we grow and transform the old blocks.

It might help you to realize that having business blocks of any kind is perfectly normal. No one has a perfect entrepreneurial mindset. There's absolutely nothing wrong with you. There's no need to fix you.

However, if you're struggling to build your business, it's probably time to take a look at this mindset stuff, no matter how challenging it might be for you. Trust me: the more you become aware of your mind gremlins, the easier it becomes for you to uncover new ones. It's just a matter of training your mind to recognize them when they pop up, and it gets easier the more you do it.

The important thing is to view them from a neutral perspective. Visibility blocks, and all types of business blocks, are neither good nor bad. They just are. And you're not bad for having them.

Perhaps make it a game to uncover your blocks. Think of it like an archaeological dig: how exciting it will be to see what you discover! That may sound silly, but the more you have fun with the process, the easier it will be.

Take action today

Review your business goals. Make a list of all the actions you'll need to take to achieve these goals, if you haven't already. If you do have the list, review it now. Then write down all the excuses that your mind comes up with—all the fears, blocks, and limiting beliefs that are triggered by your to-do list.

11

EXPLORE SECONDARY GAIN

"If you really want to do something, you'll find a way. If you don't, you'll find an excuse."

— Jim Rohn

If you're in the coaching world, you're probably already familiar with secondary gain. This is a medical term used to describe the subconscious motivation that patients may have when presenting with symptoms. For example, a person's subconscious mind might not want them to heal from chronic illness because they enjoy being cared for by a partner or family member. They know that if they get better they will no longer need to be cared for, and they may fear that the partner or family member will go back to their normal life and spend less time with them.

When we look at business visibility, the secondary gain could describe any subconscious motivation for things to stay the way they currently are, in terms of low business visibility. It's our subconscious mind's way of keeping us safe and comfortable, where we are now, inside our comfort zone. Our current situation is known; a more significant visibility situation would be something new and unknown.

Questions to ask yourself when exploring what secondary gain you may have involving business visibility (you may want to use these as journal prompts):

- Does low visibility bring anything important to your business?
- Does low visibility protect you or keep you safe in any way?
- Is there anything that low visibility doesn't allow you to do or experience that you don't like or that you're afraid of?
- Can you think of any advantage to maintaining low business visibility?
- Is there anything that you will lose, once you become more visible, that's important for you?
- Who are you as an entrepreneur without low visibility?
- How is low business visibility serving you?

Low visibility probably means fewer clients, which means you're not too busy. Perhaps you suffered from burnout in a previous career, and your subconscious is afraid that if you get too visible, your business will get too busy, and you won't be able to handle it. Better to keep things as they are.

Maybe some part of you is afraid that if you get too visible, you'll be invited onto all kinds of media opportunities: podcast, radio, and television interviews. What if you don't know how to distinguish between excellent opportunities for you and ones that aren't a good fit? What if you get interviewed by someone who asks you questions you can't answer, and you're stuck for words? It's safer to stay where you are and avoid these opportunities.

You know who you are. But who will you be if you get famous? How will you change? How will your friends and family perceive you? What if they don't like you anymore, and you end up all alone? Better to play small and stay where you are.

Perhaps you're afraid of losing your privacy if you become a big business celebrity. Maybe you're scared of online stalkers harming you or your children. Or you might be afraid of your business merely growing out of control and becoming overwhelmed. Maintaining low business visibility may protect you from any of these scenarios.

The secondary gain will be different for everyone, and it all depends on your unique fears, blocks, and limiting beliefs. It will also depend on your past business and life experiences, and your current situation. Exploring secondary gain is vital if you've done business mindset work, you've taken practical action, and you're still feeling stuck and frustrated with your visibility.

If you want to use muscle testing to explore whether or not you're currently experiencing a secondary gain in terms of your business visibility, you can muscle test on the following statements. You can read through the process in my first book, *Business Beliefs*, if you're not yet familiar with self muscle testing.

Statements to test to determine secondary gain regarding business visibility:

- I am currently experiencing secondary gain in regards to my business visibility. (*if you test strong, proceed with the next statements*)
- I have conscious knowledge of what this

secondary gain is. (*if you test strong for this, then look at the first thing that pops into your mind; if you test weak for this, proceed with the next statement*)

- This secondary gain can be found in [name of book]. (*muscle test on my* Business Beliefs *book, or use the first book that pops into your mind; if those test weak, keep going until you test strong to the correct book; from there, muscle test on the page number, then paragraph, then exact phrase from the book*)

"It's safe and appropriate for me to be visible with my business" is one of my favorite business belief statements. The concept of "safe and appropriate" is used a lot in PSYCH-K®, and I love it because it's such a powerful concept. Imagine what could be possible if you truly believed at the subconscious level that it were safe and appropriate for you to be visible with your business?

What actions would you take? How would you feel? What would your business look like? Be sure you explore any secondary gain that might get in the way of believing this. Once you identify any secondary gain, you'll need to do the subconscious work to release those beliefs.

Take Action Today

Go through this chapter again and make note of any situations that you resonate with. Answer the questions above that are designed to help you get clear on any secondary gain you might have. Muscle test to see if you are currently experiencing secondary gain.

12

THE POWER OF THE SUBCONSCIOUS MIND

"Until you make the unconscious conscious, it will direct your life and you will call it fate."

— Carl G. Jung

If you've read either of my previous books, you'll already be familiar with this chapter. You may or may not need a refresher on the importance of upgrading your business mindset at the subconscious level. If you haven't read my other books on business mindset, read on.

Let's talk a little bit about the subconscious, also known in the field of psychoanalysis as the unconscious mind. French psychologist Pierre Janet coined the term "subconscious," which is the anglicized version of the French word *subconscient*. The 18th-century German Romantic philosopher Friedrich Schelling coined the term "unconscious mind," which was later introduced into English by poet and essayist Samuel Taylor Coleridge. It was eventually popularized by Austrian psychoanalyst Sigmund

Freud, who saw the mind as being comprised of three levels:

- the conscious (10 percent of total brain function)
- the subconscious (50–60 percent)
- the unconscious (30–40 percent)

Modern-day representations of the conscious and the subconscious/unconscious minds will put the breakdown at 10–12 percent for the conscious mind and 88–90 percent for the subconscious/unconscious mind. For this book, all we need to know is that roughly 90% of total brain function does *not* take place in the conscious mind. This concept is fundamental.

You may have seen the use of an iceberg as a metaphor for the subconscious mind: just the tip of it is visible above the water, with the vast majority of the iceberg being invisible, submerged. The visible section represents your conscious mind, with the submerged part representing your subconscious mind because it is unseen, operating in the background. It's like a foundation for the conscious mind, which metaphorically sits on the surface.

Let's dig a bit deeper into the two. We'll also explore a concept known as the superconscious mind, which you may or may not be familiar with.

The conscious mind

This is the part of your mind that you're aware of throughout the day. You use it to envision what you want for your company, and you use it to set your business and life goals, to make decisions, and to plan your day. It's where logic and intellect reside, as well as your short term memory. Critical thinking skills are a part of the conscious mind, which you use to think abstractly and judge results. A big part of running your business happens in the conscious mind.

The conscious mind is time-bound and has an awareness of the past and the future. It is also said to have a minimal processing capacity: it can only focus on one to three events at a time. Again, the conscious mind makes up only about 10 percent of your total brain function.

The subconscious mind

The subconscious mind is the other 90 percent. It's responsible for all of your involuntary physical functions, such as breathing and walking. It monitors the operation of your entire body: it keeps your motor functions operating, it keeps your heart going, it makes your digestive system work, and it carries out all of the functions of your body. Take breathing. For example, you do not think about when to inhale and exhale; your subconscious mind handles that for you.

In addition to handling our essential body functions, the subconscious also handles the parts of the mind that we are not fully aware of, but which influence our actions, feelings, and emotions. It is responsible for our habits and patterns. Because the subconscious handles our long-term memory, it's in charge of storing all of our life experiences. It holds our past events, our attitudes, our beliefs, our values.

The subconscious mind is said to think literally. When you are communicating with it (you'll learn how to do that in a later chapter), you need to be crystal clear on what exactly it is that you want. The subconscious is in some ways like a small child: it takes everything you say to the letter. If you are familiar with the law of attraction, you may be aware of this concept: you need to be very specific about what you want so you can communicate the right message to the subconscious mind.

The subconscious mind is also timeless: it exists in the now. Because it only deals in the present time, it has no sense of past or future. If you work with affirmations or belief statements, they need to be in the present tense.

They also need to be positive statements, as the subconscious does not process negative commands. If you try to program a belief such as "I don't get myself into debt," the subconscious will ignore the "don't" and instead will hear "I get myself into debt." Think about it this way: if you're in London and you want to visit Covent Garden, you won't get good results by walking up to someone and saying "Please don't give me directions to Buckingham Palace." You'd want to specifically ask for directions on how to get to Covent Garden because that's where you want to go. Focus on what you do want, not on what you don't want.

Our subconscious is also responsible for our self-sabotage. It has all this information based on our life experiences stored in its long term memory, and it's in charge of self-preservation. This means that—based on the beliefs it holds—it can sometimes make somewhat illogical decisions or lead us to take irrational action in its effort to keep us safe and secure.

While this can be incredibly frustrating, it's important to remember that our subconscious is merely trying to help. If a person "accidentally" misses a deadline to apply for a speaking engagement, that might simply have been their subconscious trying to help them avoid public humiliation. Like when they stood up in front of the class in fifth grade to give a presentation and then tripped and fell, causing the entire class to burst out in laughter.

The subconscious mind is a powerhouse: it does so much, and it does it automatically, working in the background. It is not something that we usually control. However, it is something that we *can* control: instead of falling victim to the often unhelpful guidance of our subconscious, which may be operating on old programs, we have ways of programming new beliefs into the subconscious.

When I talk about "deep mindset work," this is what I mean: reprogramming new beliefs into our subconscious. This process is how I work with myself and with other people to transform beliefs and mindset. Unfortunately, most people are unfamiliar with these types of techniques, and therefore this is something that they do not do on a day to day basis. Most of us function with the subconscious running its programs automatically, even when they no longer serve us.

The superconscious mind

Some spiritual belief systems acknowledge a third part of the mind, known as the superconscious or higher self. You may know this by another term, such as the authentic self, the divine self, the higher mind, universal consciousness, or the soul. If you don't believe in this concept, that's fine, and you can move right along to the next section. I need to address this, but you don't have to believe in it yourself. You'll still get the results from working with your subconscious mind.

The superconscious mind, or higher self, is the core of who you are as an individual. It knows your path to success, your life purpose, your life passion. It knows where you've come from and where you're going. It's in charge of delivering wise guidance to you in the form of your intuition or gut feeling. If you believe in a higher power, you may see it as being your connection with the Divine, Source, Spirit, God, Goddess, or whatever you call this spiritual power.

The superconscious can also be accessed to get wisdom regarding our mindset and the beliefs that we need to have to achieve our goals—more on that in a bit.

Take action today

What are your thoughts about all this? Take a few minutes to think about—or to journal on—your current relationship with your conscious, subconscious, and superconscious minds. Are you truly in touch with each aspect of yourself? Do you feel better connected to one part of your mind than to the others? Do you believe in the concept of the superconscious mind? If so, what do you call it?

On the podcast

You can find the full list of podcast episodes here:
www.hollyworton.com/podcast

- 272 Holly Worton ~ Mindset: Why It Isn't About Positive Thinking

13

TRANSFORM YOUR SUBCONSCIOUS MINDSET

"At the end of the day, you are the only one that is limiting your ability to dream, or to actually execute on your dreams. Don't let yourself get in the way of that."

— Falon Fatemi

The first step is to get clear on what you want (Chapter 5). Next, become aware of your visibility fears, blocks, and limiting beliefs (Chapters 6, 7, 8, and 9). Then, you need to do the work to transform your beliefs at the subconscious level. The power of awareness helps us do this deeper work to upgrade our business mindset and release our visibility blocks.

Remember when I talked about how powerful the subconscious mind was in the previous chapter? We can now harness the power of the subconscious mind so we can change these fears, blocks, and limiting beliefs into business-enhancing beliefs at that deep level. This will help us more easily take the actions we need to take to increase our business visibility.

There are many ways you could do this: by working with a practitioner or therapist or by doing the work with yourself. I recommend a combination of the two: I regularly use PSYCH-K® with myself to transform my business mindset, but I also work with another PSYCH-K® facilitator to help me uncover my blocks and get to the core of what's going on for me.

And occasionally, I have some other type of session, like EFT™ (Emotional Freedom Techniques), Resonance Repatterning®, or TRE® (Trauma Release Exercises) to mix it up and approach my mindset from a different angle and release trauma differently.

I also believe that it's essential to mix the mindset work with practical action, which is where a business coach or mentor comes in. Whenever I speak with Lisa Wechtenhiser, my business coach/mentor, each session brings up loads of things to work on, and I'm not just talking about practical action steps. Having a new action plan will usually bring up fears, blocks, and other mindset stuff for me to work on.

As I've said before, you must find the technique that works best for you. That could be PSYCH-K®, or it could be NLP (Neuro-linguistic Programming), EFT™, TAT® (Tapas Acupressure Technique®), hypnotherapy, Resonance Repatterning®, ThetaHealing®, or something else. You might need to try a few different techniques before you find what works for you. I include PSYCH-K® as an example in a lot of my stories because I've tried so many different methods, and that's what I most enjoy using. It's fast, easy, and it's easy to learn.

You may be wondering: what if you can't find the best technique or practitioner for you? Trust me, you will. You might have to try a handful of different modalities and techniques and maybe another handful of practitioners or facilitators, but you'll get there. Trust that you'll find the way.

For example, with PSYCH-K®, I first saw a facilitator who talked me out of having a PSYCH-K® session and using a different technique instead—ThetaHealing®. While I enjoyed the session, I wanted to try PSYCH-K® because that was the process that had been recommended to me.

Then I saw a facilitatory who wasn't a good fit for me. I saw her for one session, and then never returned. I tried emailing another one, but she replied, saying that she didn't feel comfortable working with me on the issues I wanted to work on.

Finally, I saw another PSYCH-K® facilitator who blended it with several different techniques. I never returned to her because I had already booked my Basic Workshop for later that month. Since then, I've met several PSYCH-K® facilitators who are a perfect fit for me to work with. I link to them in Chapter 15, so you can work with them if you like—they all do online sessions, so it doesn't matter where you are in the world.

Even when you've found the right technique for you, it can take time to find the best professional to work with. Be patient. It will happen.

If you don't have lots of money to invest in trying all of these different techniques and practitioners, you can approach people about doing a swap session with you. I know many business mentors speak against this, but if it's the only way for you to get the sessions you need and want, then I think it's worth trying.

You can also use EFT™ scripts that are available online. While pre-written scripts are no substitute for working with a trained practitioner, they can be a good start if you're on a low budget. Just search for them online or on

YouTube, where you can find instructional videos that will walk you through each step.

I hope you've found this book to be useful. I've tried to keep it short, simple, and actionable, so you can quickly and easily identify the blocks that keep you stuck in your business. Awareness is the just first step: actually changing your beliefs at the subconscious is vital if you want to upgrade your business mindset.

Think about the following: what does it cost you to avoid doing this deep mindset work? It's so easy to put off and just keep doing what you've been doing so far. After all, it keeps you safe within your comfort zone! But what will your business be like six months from now if you don't take action? If you don't get clarity on what mindset shifts you need to make? What will your business be like if you don't make those changes?

Next, we're going to talk about how to take inspired action to create changes in your business.

On the podcast

You can find the full list of podcast episodes here: www.hollyworton.com/podcast

- 333 Do You Have a Fixed Mindset or a Growth Mindset? (now with downloadable transcript!)
- 300 Celebrating 300 Episodes of Mindset, Growth, and Change! (now with downloadable transcript!)
- 295 Sharon Lock ~ How to Make Mindset Work a Habit (now with downloadable transcript!)
- 276 How to Create Your Own Personal Formula

For Mindset Work & Healing (now with downloadable transcript!)

- 272 Mindset: Why It *Isn't* About Positive Thinking (now with downloadable transcript!)
- 270 Why Mindset Matters (now with downloadable transcript!)
- 245 How to Spring Clean Your Business + Mindset (now with downloadable transcript!)
- 230 How to Make Mindset Work a Habit (now with downloadable transcript!)
- 192 Get the Mindset You Need to Make a Big Impact (now with downloadable transcript!)
- 181 Jo Casey + Holly ~ Is Mindset Important in Business, or Is It Just an Excuse to Avoid Action?
- 157 How to Increase Your Visibility by Transforming Your Mindset
- 136 Why You Can't Afford to Ignore Your Business Mindset
- 115 How to Get the Right Mindset for Your Business

14

TAKE INSPIRED ACTION

"You gain strength, courage and confidence by every experience in which you really stop to look fear in the face. You are able to say to yourself, "I lived through this horror. I can take the next thing that comes along." You must do the thing you think you cannot do."

— ELEANOR ROOSEVELT

Are you wondering exactly what you need to do now? It's easy: I've broken it all down into five easy action steps. This is where you need to be ready, willing, and able to do the work. Your mindset won't upgrade on its own, and your business won't build itself without work.

And just reading this book isn't enough, either. Hopefully you've been making notes and journaling as you've been reading, but if you haven't, you can always go back and do it now. Theory won't get you changes; action will.

Transforming our mindset doesn't need to be difficult, but it isn't exactly magic. It does require an investment of time and action, and probably money in most cases. We've got to take action and we've got to put the time in to do the work.

Here's how to get started:

1. Get clear on what you want.
2. Identify the core fears, blocks, and limiting beliefs that you need to shift in your business mindset, using the methods and questions described in this book. If you want or need even more clarity, get my first book, *Business Beliefs*, and worth through that. There's a whole list of visibility blocks in there, and you'll learn how to test to see whether or not your subconscious mind holds a particular belief.
3. Find the best technique for you to change your mindset at the subconscious level. You may already know what that is, or it may take time to find what works for you. Be patient, and keep trying.
4. Find the best practitioner or facilitator to help you with this mindset transformation, or do the work yourself. Maybe you've found the best technique for you, but the first person you see doesn't feel like a good fit. That's fine...keep trying. Remember my story about finding the right PSYCH-K® facilitator for me.
5. Do the inner work to transform your mindset.
6. Take practical action to reinforce your mindset transformation. Most PSYCH-K® facilitators will help you create an action plan at the end of each session. If the person you see does not help you

to create an action plan, then do it yourself, either alone or with your business coach/mentor.

7. Repeat. Business is like going up a spiral staircase: one step is practical action, and the other is mindset work. Step by step, you grow your business and move toward achieving your big business vision.

I've mentioned it before, but it's important for me to clarify once again that this work never ends. If you're committed to growing your business and to growing as an individual, you'll keep uncovering new blocks as you evolve. The good news is that, in my experience, you need to do less and less work as you declutter limiting beliefs.

When I first trained in PSYCH-K®, I balanced 10-20 beliefs *every single day*. Now, I probably work with myself once a week or once every ten days. I keep a notebook where I write down everything I want to work on, and when I have time to have a session with myself, I do the work.

The more you declutter, the more limiting beliefs you'll uncover, and eventually you'll notice that you have less to clear up. For a while, it may feel like it's all bubbling up to the surface. It can seem messy.

That's because you're becoming increasingly aware of the stuff that you need to work on. After a time, you'll have cleared the most important stuff and you won't need to do as much work. Imagine pouring fresh water into a glass of dirty water. The more clean water you pour into it, the more the water in the glass clears up. Eventually, it's all clean, fresh water.

I hesitated to use that as an example. I think it's a great visual, but I don't want you to think that business blocks as something that's dirty. Yes, they're undesirable, but as I said earlier, they're also neutral. They're neither good nor bad.

Finding the best technique for you may involve trial and error, as will finding the best practitioner or facilitator for you. If something doesn't feel quite right, then don't go back for another session. Listen to your gut feeling on this, and if you don't see changes fairly soon after your first session or first couple of sessions, you might want to re-evaluate whether you've found the best method or best practitioner for you. (You also might have resistance to change, but any experienced practitioner or facilitator can help you if this is the case.)

Change can be very quick when you're working at the subconscious level, so there's no need to attend weekly sessions for months before seeing results. Stay alert, and pay attention to how your life and business are different since you started doing the mindset work. Sometimes big changes occur, but people don't notice them, because things are going well and they're no longer experiencing whatever it was that they wanted to let go of.

It helps to write things down. That's part of the reason why I send all of my new clients a questionnaire: it helps them get clarity on what they want to work on and it helps me save time during the actual session by getting lots of background information. But it also gives us a point of reference so that we can compare how the person was feeling and what they were experiencing when we first started working to what's going on after we've done some work together.

"I'm ready, willing, and able to be visible with my business" is another one of my favorite business belief statements. This is a powerful statement that expresses that you are stepping into your power and choosing to be visible. You may believe, with your conscious mind, that you are ready, willing, and able to be visible with your business. But is your subconscious mind on board with that? If not, it's easy enough to change your beliefs around this. And once your subconscious is on board, it makes it easy and effortless to take inspired action to become more visible with your business.

In the next chapter, I talk a little bit about how you can work with a professional if you feel drawn to do so. Even if you don't think you have the budget to work with someone at this time, I encourage you to read through it anyway, so you can at least have some point of comparison to other professionals that you may choose to work with in the future. It helps to have an idea of how different people work so you can find what's best for you.

Remember...*you* know what's best for you! There's a reason I keep saying this: we can have the tendency to give our power away to others, but deep down, *you're* the one who knows what's best. Go with your intuition or with what your heart says. That's your higher self speaking to you and checking in to let you know which option is right for you.

15

NEED MORE HELP?

"Whether it's your family, friends, community that you connect with, don't be afraid to reach out. That's my biggest advice that I can say for anyone going through any kind of obstacle or trials or tribulations. Don't be afraid to reach out and ask questions. Ask for help, because you never know where you'll find it."

— VANESSA WILLIAMS

Feeling stuck? If you've read this book, and are still feeling like you need more help engaging the power of your inner wisdom, read on. Or perhaps you've taken the five inspired action steps, and you uncovered some fears, blocks, or limiting beliefs that have gotten in the way of you honing your business intuition. If that's the case, it's time to get help.

Is this you?

Are you a coach, a healer, or a holistic therapist? Maybe you've got another type of business, and you're on a mission to change the world through the work that you do. You may be just starting out in business, or you may be in the process of growing your existing business.

But you've hit a rough spot. You've done all the business and marketing training, but somehow things just aren't flowing for you. You're feeling stuck. Frustrated.

All you want is more clients so you can help more people (and, let's face it, make a decent living from your business). You're starting to realize that being successful in business isn't just about knowing how to market and run a business. It's also about your mindset: making sure that your beliefs and your inner dialogue are aligned with your vision and goals.

But it's not always that easy, is it?

Maybe you're struggling with:

- Lack of confidence, which leads to you procrastinating on getting your Most Important Tasks completed.
- Fear that people won't get what you do. They won't want it, or else they won't be willing to pay you for it.
- Issues around visibility and fear of standing out in the online crowd.
- Fear of overwhelm if you actually do attract all the clients you want and build a thriving business.
- Getting started with social media marketing,

speaking, videos, and webinars. . .the thought of any of this makes you cringe.

- Believing you have something really valuable to offer. I mean, you know you do, but. . .do you really?

Have you ever experienced any of this?

If so, you're not alone. I really struggled with this stuff when I started my second business, and my business suffered. Fortunately, I found an easy solution: one that's fast, effective, and painless. It transformed my business and it transformed my life.

Imagine how it would feel if:

- You only attracted great clients: people who know what they want and they value what you do.
- You felt nourished and fulfilled by your business, confident that you were making a difference in the world, client by client.
- You had a tribe of raving fans who were eager to sign up for your new product or service launches.
- You had a clear vision for your business that was totally aligned with your purpose: 100% you.
- Your business felt like it was in flow, with a regular stream of clients ready to invest in what you have to offer.

Sound good?

This is what I want for you. I want to help purpose-driven women entrepreneurs create the business of their dreams that allows them to live the lifestyle they want.

As I mentioned earlier in the book, I've stepped back from doing one-to-one sessions so I can focus on my writing. However, I do offer occasional sessions to my Patrons in my Patreon community.

Head over to www.patreon.com/hollyworton and check it out. Please email if you have any questions:

holly@hollyworton.com.

Podcast

As you've seen at the end of some chapters, I've got many podcast episodes on mindset. This is a great way to deepen your understanding of your own mindset, and find new ways of transforming your business beliefs. Most podcast episodes have full transcripts available on the website, either to read directly or as a free pdf download (no email required).

One-to-one work

If you're ready to get started with one-to-one sessions right now, I have some recommendations for you. These are five women that I trust completely and often go to for sessions myself. They all work online via Skype/Zoom.

I highly recommend these five facilitators:

- Cara Wilde: http://carawilde.com
- Cazzie Dare: https://yearning4learning.co.uk/

- Claire Baker: http://happyhealthyempowered.com/
- Jo Trewartha: http://freeyourmindsolutions.com/
- Sharon Lock: http://sharonlock.com

Take Action Today

1. Check out my Patreon and see if you're interested in joining me there.
2. Subscribe to my podcast (Into the Woods with Holly Worton) and listen to the episodes on mindset.
3. Find a process or technique that resonates with you and a facilitator to have sessions with.
4. Once you find a technique that you love, train in it so you can use it to work with yourself.
5. If you want to do a deep dive into your business beliefs, buy the *Business Visibility* workbook.

16

TESTIMONIALS

I'm including testimonials from my clients so you can get an idea of the results you can achieve from doing work to transform your mindset at the subconscious level. Again, I rarely do one-to-one sessions, so this isn't about me trying to sell to you. It's about new possibilities. Remember, find the best method to use for *you*, and find the best professional for *you*. There's no one solution for everyone.

> I was so hopeful for results when I signed on with Holly, as I opened a business about 6 months prior. My financial and physical stress were through the roof, until Holly guided me to changing the appropriate belief statements. I have **no more chest pain, no more heavyweight stress** on my shoulders, and **my most recent month's collections at the office was $80,000! I am a magnet for money and success!** Thank you Holly! xo
>
> — Elizabeth D. Walker DMD, MSD

I have undertaken more traditional coaching before and found it useful but I wanted to really tap into a deeper way of working—particularly accessing the subconscious level. **I found the HEW process really powerful** during each session and focussing on how I felt during the session (and afterwards) helped tap me into other things. My instinct was to work with Holly because I resonate with a lot of the points she makes in her videos and podcast and she is a really warm person. It was also important to me that I felt like Holly was working through a lot of the same issues that were coming up for me. This authenticity was really important to me. I would definitely do more work with Holly in the future and would recommend working with her to others.

— Louisa Whitney

When I first found Holly, I was struggling to get my business to a place of success. I had the foundation in place, and had done all the "right" things, but somehow, it still wasn't working . . . for me. I felt like I had a mindset limitation holding me back. After my initial meeting with Holly, even before our first working session, I received $16K in unexpected personal income—debts repaid, a royalty check, a bank refund . . . after only two working sessions, I booked $43K in sales for my business, and I quit my job. That was a dream I had held for over two years, and had been working for. It wasn't magic, I put the work in, had a funnel, ads and sales conversations all set, but the results from working with Holly were literally overnight, and amazing. So much so, that had you told me that this would be happening . . . to me . . . I would never have believed you. . . in a million years. Working with Holly is seriously one of the best investments in my business and my life, that I have ever made. Thanks Holly.

— Julie Languille

Working with you has made a huge difference. In fact, I think it's made all the difference. Even if things don't feel comfortable I still persevere.

— Natasha Mann

I've had some really beneficial results from the session. The changing of beliefs about myself is really working. For the first time since I started working for myself I have confidence in the value of my services and the prices I'm quoting. It's an amazing process.

— Gill Hunt

Holly's assumption of unlimited potential and possibilities in her clients, gives her a laser focused ability to spot false limitations. Holly combines her skills with compassion and sensitivity which allows you to share yourself at a deep level. Her passion for PSYCH-K and her commitment to walk her talk makes her a leader in field. I recommend working with her in a heart beat.

— Cara Wilde

Since working with Holly and fully owning what I'm really about my business has been going through a big change. The transformation and higher consciousness work to help entrepreneurs find their natural Flow and abundance is now taking centre stage.

It's not only easier to share what I do now because I'm just being myself, but I created a successful online programme called The Flow Project, I've been interviewed for podcasts and invited to speak at events on the topic, and opportunities to collaborate on projects incorporating spirituality in business are opening up all the time! It feels like I turned a major corner and my business has become really exciting!

— Cathy Ballard

Holly, PSYCH-K and more importantly your kind, generous way of practicing it have been fundamental in my decluttering once and for all. OMG the peace I feel is amazing. What else can I say but THANK YOU.

You have really helped me to see and work on some fundamental issues that have kept me from moving forward with my business and my life. YOU are the bomb.

— Bibi F.

Despite over the years of my own journey of personal growth and working on myself there was one major thing that just wasn't shifting, and it was a constant negative effect on my life that I could never quite break free of despite having tried lots of things. The weird thing is that the issues that Holly worked with me on just sort of dissolved. These were big issues of a traumatic nature that it felt like my emotional and physical body just didn't want to let go of—but after working with Holly these things just melted away. What's amazing is how quickly I saw this profound change.

— Catherine Watkin

I feel more confident that I will be able to develop and achieve my dream business and attract my ideal clients. I also am experiencing more clarity about how to use social media and know that I will overcome any blocks or obstacles. Since the session I do not feel that sense of fear and paralysis when I start to approach the social media format or platforms. I feel and know the changes on a physical, emotional, energetic and spiritual level. This was the best thing I could have done for myself and my business.

— Jacqueline Conroy

Holly's process is absolutely phenomenal. I can hardly believe **how quickly things start to change** after we have a session— **I've seen results as soon as hours after working with her**! Somehow after we clear what needs to be cleared and call in what I desire I see opportunities that I missed before, move forward on ideas that I've been sitting on, and say yes to exactly the right things. It's like during a session with Holly **I realign my energy to match what I want to experience** – and so when we're done what I want can't help but appear in my world. **Absolutely magical**, do your future self a big favor and book in with Holly now!

— Joanna Hennon

BUSINESS INTUITION

TOOLS TO HELP YOU TRUST YOUR OWN INSTINCTS, CONNECT WITH YOUR INNER COMPASS, AND EASILY MAKE THE RIGHT DECISIONS

"Intuition is seeing with the soul."

— Dean Koontz

First of all, what is intuition? It is defined as "the ability to understand something instinctively, without the need for conscious reasoning." It has also been described as "a thing that one knows or considers likely from instinctive feeling rather than conscious reasoning." Business intuition can be defined as business knowledge that one holds, based on instinctive feeling rather than conscious reasoning.

It's also known as:

- Awareness
- Feeling
- Funny feeling (especially if the intuitive message is perceived as negative)

- Gut feeling
- Heart (though some people also use this term to refer to their emotions, which is different)
- Higher wisdom
- Hunch
- Inner compass
- Inner voice
- Insight
- Instinct
- Little voice
- Perception
- Sixth sense
- Third eye
- True north

I could go on, but I decided to limit the list to some of the more common terms. You may have another word for intuition, and if you do, please continue to use that when you're thinking about it. There's no need to use someone else's terminology if you've got something else that fits better for you.

Intuition is not a conscious process, and it is not a step-by-step procedure using logic, reasoning, or common sense. It's quick, and it usually involves ideas, thoughts, or messages that suddenly pop into your head. Unfortunately, if you haven't trained yourself to grab onto these messages and take action on their advice, they can easily slip away, smothered by the voice of reason, otherwise known as your conscious mind or your head.

Where does intuition come from?

We could probably debate this for days, and I'm sure everyone has their own opinion on where intuition originates. I'm going to start with where I think it *doesn't* come from.

If you do a quick online search, you'll find many people claiming that intuition comes from knowledge stored in your subconscious mind. However, in my experience working with the subconscious mind, I have found that unless we've done lots of work to reprogram enhancing beliefs into our subconscious, it's often running on old programs that no longer serve us. These old programs show up in the form of fears and limiting beliefs that keep us stuck safely inside our comfort zone, making it harder for us to take new actions that will help us grow our business.

While our intuition may stem from our unconscious mind, I think it's more likely that it comes from what PSYCH-K® calls the *super*conscious mind, which you may refer to as your higher self, your soul, your spirit, your divine self, or perhaps something else entirely. The superconscious mind, or higher self, sees the big picture of your life and sends you messages based on your best interest and highest good, and not on what your ego wants.

This is why I (and many others) believe that the wisdom we get from our intuitive messages is so infallible, and why the quote I included earlier from Rachel Wolchin states that "your gut is always right." The way I see it, the messages from our higher selves can't be wrong, and they will always guide you in the right direction.

How does our intuition speak to us?

Well, it's different for everyone. I mostly get gut feelings, but I also get voices in my head. I know that sounds a little crazy, so please stick with me here. It's the good kind of voices.

I'm a very visual person, and in terms of my learning preferences (visual, auditory, and kinesthetic), I'm visual/kinesthetic. I prefer to learn by reading things, and also by doing them. I'm not very auditory, meaning that I don't learn best by listening to things like lectures or podcasts or audiobooks, even though I enjoy listening to them. The information doesn't stick when I hear it.

So it doesn't make sense that my intuition speaks to me with words that I hear, but that's how it usually works for me. I also get that gut feeling, which may relate to my kinesthetic learning preference. From my experience, there's not a definite crossover between learning preference and the voice of your intuition.

So if you're a strong auditory learner, your intuition may speak to you differently. Be open to the possibility of receiving messages in whatever way, shape, or form your inner wisdom chooses to send to you. You may be surprised.

I'm going to talk a little bit about the clair senses now. We often hear talk of these in terms of psychic ability, which you may or may not believe in. And if you don't, that's perfectly fine, and belief in psychic ability is not necessary for you to understand these concepts.

These clair senses are also ways in which our intuition can speak to us, so let's take a look at them. They're like the different "languages" that our intuition uses. You know how we can communicate with each other using the spoken word, the written word, or with sign language? Your intuition also uses verbal, nonverbal, and visual communication.

There are three primary clair senses that you're probably familiar with, and four minor senses that may be new to you. Let's explore these different languages.

Clairvoyance

I can't remember ever experiencing this, despite being a highly visual person. This particular "language" or method of communication involves presenting you with visual cues or symbols. You might get a specific mental image that will give you clues as to what your intuition is trying to tell you. They may come to you during meditation, or they may pop into your head during the day.

Clairaudience

This is one of the languages my intuition uses to speak to me. I'll hear words, either single words or phrases, that pop up in my mind. Often I'll get these messages during a quiet moment when I'm in between tasks. They also can come when I'm doing some kind of repetitive exercise, like running or walking, where I can quickly get into the zone, a mental state where I'm relaxed and not thinking about anything in particular.

Have you ever heard of "shower thoughts?" Shower thoughts refer to any idea you might have while carrying out a routine task like showering, driving, or daydreaming. Sometimes they're random, silly connections that your brain makes (I'm thinking of the subreddit /r/showerthoughts on the Reddit.com website, which you might find entertaining), but often they're useful bits of inner wisdom.

Clairsentience

This is another one of the languages my intuition uses to speak to me. I get a gut feeling about something. It could be a message that something is right or wrong for me, or that I should or should not do something. Or I could get a feeling when I see a particular object or person that makes me stop and pause, allowing more information to come to me via clairaudience.

This communication method involves getting a feeling somewhere in your body, without any outer stimuli to trigger that feeling. It could be in your gut, or it could involve chills all over your body. Have you ever gotten goosebumps when someone said something that resonated with you? This is your inner wisdom's way of saying, "Hey! Pay attention."

Clairempathy

This may relate to clairsentience, or that gut feeling that I get. I usually get very, very strong first impressions of people, and they're always right. Whenever I've allowed my head to override that first impression, it always leads to trouble.

Clairempathy allows us to sense or feel the attitudes, emotions, or beliefs of another person. It's like you feel their energy or vibration, and that can give you useful information about that person. This could be your intuition's way of giving you valuable details that your conscious mind might not pick up.

Clairgustance

This is an odd one: it involves tasting a substance or food without having anything in your mouth. Because this is such a strange sensation, it may be your intuition telling you to pay attention, or it may be a way of providing some type of (tasty) symbol that directly relates to the message you need to receive. It might also be a way of letting you know whether something is right (delicious) or wrong (not delicious) for you. This is purely speculation because I've never experienced this sensation.

Clairscent

This is precisely what it sounds like: smelling a fragrance or an odor that is not present in your surroundings. I've experienced this before, for example, smelling a familiar perfume that someone I know wears, despite them not being present, but I've never been able to relate it to a particular message. Again, this may be another way of your intuition getting your attention or sending you a direct message.

I also went through a period of time where I would randomly smell something burning—when in fact there was nothing on fire. I always had the sensation that something was trying to get my attention, and perhaps it was simply my intuition saying, "Hey!"

Clairtangency

In psychic terms, this usually refers to someone who can handle an object or touch something and receive information about that object. In terms of intuition, this could mean touching a thing and receiving some type of message from your intuition, either about that object or about something completely unrelated. The object might serve as a trigger for your intuition to speak to you, giving you a much clearer message via clairvoyance, clairaudience, or clairsentience.

Take Action Today

As you read through the different clair senses, which ones sounded familiar? Which of the senses have you experienced in your own life? Write this down in your journal, along with some times when you've experienced your intuition speaking to you in these ways.

On the podcast

You can find the full list of podcast episodes here:
www.hollyworton.com/podcast

- 292 Joanna Hennon + Holly ~ What's Better: Spirit Guides or Tapping into Your Intuition? Part II (now with downloadable transcript!)
- 290 Jo Casey + Holly ~ What's Better: Spirit Guides or Tapping into Your Intuition? (now with downloadable transcript!)
- 235 Joanna Hennon + Holly ~ How to Find the Right Balance Between Structure and Intuition (now with downloadable transcript!)
- 162 Tap Into Your Intuition to Make Your Business Easier
- 141 Caroline Frenette ~ How to Master Your Intuition to Create Quantum Leaps in Business
- 83 How to Follow Your Creative Intuition, with Flora Bowley
- 79 How to Tap Into Your Intuition & Add Magic to Your Business, with Fifi Mills

ABOUT THE AUTHOR

Holly Worton is a podcaster and nine times published author. Her 2019 book, *If Trees Could Talk: Life Lessons from the Wisdom of the Woods*, went straight to the top of 16 Amazon bestseller lists, and she has been featured on BBC Radio Scotland and on prime time national television in the UK – on ITV's This Morning.

She helps people get to know themselves better through connecting with Nature, so they can feel happier and more fulfilled. Holly enjoys spending time outdoors, walking long-distance trails and exploring Britain's sacred sites. She's originally from California and now lives in the Surrey Hills, but has also lived in Spain, Costa Rica, Mexico, Chile, and Argentina. Holly is a member of the Druid order OBOD.

Holly ran her first business for ten years, building it up to become a multi-million-dollar enterprise. When she went into the coaching world she was confident that she had the business and marketing skills she needed to set up a new company. And she did – but she struggled to grow her new venture quickly because she encountered fears, blocks, and limiting beliefs that she didn't even know she had.

She discovered that pushing forward and taking action just wasn't enough. She needed to transform her mindset and release her blocks, as this was the only way to take the *right* actions to move her new business forward. Thus began her journey of intense personal development through deep mindset work, which transformed her existing coaching business into a focus on helping people with their business mindset.

Eventually, she realized that she wanted to devote her time to helping people through her writing, and she let go of her mindset business to focus on her books. Now, Holly continues to write about mindset, long-distance walking, and connecting to Nature.

Podcast

You can find her podcast on Apple Podcasts, or wherever you listen to podcasts. Links to subscribe, as well as the full list of episodes, can be found here: http://www.hollyworton.com/podcast/.

Patreon

You can join her online community where you can receive the benefits of her done-for-you mindset work, and also get discounts on one-to-one sessions, by joining her on Patreon: https://www.patreon.com/hollyworton.

Books

You can find her other books, including her books on nature, walking long-distance trails and business mindset, wherever you purchased this book.

Newsletter

Finally, you can stay in touch by subscribing to her newsletter on her main website: http://www.hollyworton.com/.

amazon.com/author/hollyworton
facebook.com/HollyWortonPage
twitter.com/hollyworton
instagram.com/hollyworton
goodreads.com/HollyWorton
bookbub.com/profile/holly-worton

ALSO BY HOLLY E. WORTON

Business Mindset series

Business Beliefs: Upgrade Your Mindset to Overcome Self Sabotage, Achieve Your Goals, and Transform Your Business (and Life)

Business Beliefs: A Companion Workbook

Business Blocks: Transform Your Self-Sabotaging Mind Gremlins, Awaken Your Inner Mentor, and Allow Your Business Brilliance to Shine

Business Blocks: A Companion Workbook

Business Intuition: Tools to Help You Trust Your Own Instincts, Connect with Your Inner Compass, and Easily Make the Right Decisions

Business Intuition: A Companion Workbook

Business Visibility: A Companion Workbook

Into the Woods Short Reads

How to Add More Adventure to Your Life

How to Practice Self-Love: Actual Steps You Can Take To Love Yourself More

How to Practice Self Care: Even When You Think You're Too Busy

How to Develop Your Own Inner Compass: Learn to Trust Yourself and Easily Make the Best Decisions

Nature books

If Trees Could Talk: Life Lessons from the Wisdom of the Woods

If Trees Could Talk: Life Lessons from the Wisdom of the Woods — A Companion Workbook

Walking books

Alone on the South Downs Way: A Tale of Two Journeys from Winchester to Eastbourne

Walking the Downs Link: Planning Guide & Reflections on Walking from St. Martha's Hill to Shoreham-by-Sea

Alone on the Ridgeway: One Woman's Solo Journey from Avebury to Ivinghoe Beacon

Walking the Wey-South Path: Planning Guide & Reflections on Walking from Guildford to Amberley

A REQUEST

If you enjoyed this book, please review it online. It takes just a couple of minutes to write a quick review. It would mean the world to me! Good reviews help other readers to discover new books.

Thank you, thank you, thank you.